Calling Yankees to Florida

Harriet Beecher Stowe's Forgotten Tourist Articles

Introduced and Edited
by
John T. Foster Jr. and Sarah Whitmer Foster

Calling Yankees to Florida
Harriet Beecher Stowe's Forgotten Tourist Articles

ISBN 10: 1-886104-53-0
ISBN 13: 978-1-886104-53-2

The Florida Historical Society Press
435 Brevard Avenue
Cocoa, FL 32922
www.myfloridahistory.org/fhspress

DEDICATION

The idea for this work is a response to a question asked by R. E. Lemon.

To R. E. Lemon,
whose wisdom changes lives.

Johnson's 1864 Map of Florida depicting the state during Harriet Beecher Stowe's era. Florida Historical Society.

Table of Contents

List of Illustrations

> Stowe's Florida ventures have been treated [by Stowe scholars] as a private affair, begun in the effort to rehabilitate an alcoholic son and continued as a seasonal escape from northern winters. Her reform efforts have not been credited with producing significant results, and the extent of her connections with reform circles in Florida has been overlooked.
>
> —Patricia R. Hill,
> "Beechers, Stowes, and Yankee Strangers:
> The Transformation of Florida,"
> *Journal of American History*, June 2000, 237.

Preface

Probably few members of the public now know that the famous author and abolitionist Harriet Beecher Stowe owned a Florida house from which she wrote rhapsodic articles about the state during the years 1867-1881. All of these were published separately, mostly in newspapers and other periodicals. Some ended up as part of a series published as a once well-known book—*Palmetto-Leaves*—but many more of her articles were never collected. It is from these previously uncompiled articles and essays that we have assembled this work.

The novelist truly loved Florida and for much of her time in the state she was free to be herself. Stowe found inspiration in Florida's brilliant colors as well as wonder in her giant oak trees and the new bright foliage of the cypress trees in a nearby swamp. She showed remarkable powers of observation, even noticing the difference between living moss, seeing it as "delicate, pearly, greenish white," and the uniform gray of the dead moss. Having found amazing beauty, she described it with joy.

As a writer who attracted many of Florida's first tourists, her approach often paralleled that of modern ecotourism. Her father, the famous minister Lyman Beecher, believed that Stowe was "a genius" and in writing from and about Florida she showed wonderful flashes of those remarkable talents. We hope the readers will enjoy them as much as we have.

These articles offer much more than pleasure, however—a realization that even few scholars have had. Stowe's biographers normally attach little historical significance to them. To them, the novelist just seemed to be escaping from dreadful weather and poorly heated houses. For most of the twentieth century little emerged from historians in Florida to suggest otherwise. Stowe's annual trips south began in 1867 and continued until her husband's health collapsed in 1884, with the majority of those years occurring during Reconstruction. Historians in Florida interpretively followed the pattern commonly given to the rest of the South. The Reconstruction was dismissed as an age of corrupt Carpetbaggers who colluded with newly freed African Americans to oppress traditional Southerners. The supposed wrongs gave rise to the Ku Klux Klan and political efforts to recover political control. "Redemption" (the recovery of state and local control) happened in the wake of the election of 1876, when Democrats accepted the election of Rutherford B. Hayes as President and they attained the governorships of Florida, Louisiana, and South Carolina. Historians wrote accounts that movie director D. W. Griffith used in his film "Birth of a Nation."

A reconsideration of this interpretation began with Jerrell H. Shofner's book, *Nor is it Over Yet: Florida in the Reconstruction Era.* Shofner began the process of carefully examining what had actually taken place, indicating that positive events had occurred. The state's modern public school system, for example, with districts based upon counties, began in the period. He also documented that many of the unsuccessful attempts to impeach Florida governor Harrison Reed actually came from a corrupt faction in the Republican Party. The active support of many Southerners and Democrats was crucial to the state's first Republican chief executive staying in office. Harrison Reed was not a part of the radical wing of his party.

While Shofner's work began the process of reevaluating the era as it affected Florida, the same process occurred nationally with Eric

Foner's classic work, *Reconstruction: America's Unfinished Revolution*. The reality of the era was very different from the simplistic and prejudicial myths woven by earlier historians. The period was, in fact, a failed effort to make democracy real for everyone—and its failure condemned African Americans to an often brutal, second-class citizenship. The modern Civil Rights Movement emerged in the twentieth century as a direct consequence of the events of the 1860s and 1870s. The validity of both Foner's work and Shofner's has led to innumerable articles, monographs, and books correcting the distortions of the past.

Writings about Harriet Beecher Stowe in Florida also cover the eras before and after the period covered by Shofner. In 1958, Mary B. Graff wrote *Mandarin on the St. Johns*, chronicling the activities of Stowe and her husband in the context of the history of a small village. Graff found, not surprisingly, that they had an impact upon the community by their efforts to establish a church. The village ended up with a permanent place of worship in 1883 and, in 1916, a Tiffany window to commemorate the efforts of Harriet Beecher Stowe and her husband. While Graff was aware of the novelist's brother serving in statewide office and the publication of a family article in a periodical, *The Semi-Tropical*, she never connects them. Charles Beecher served as the State Superintendent of Public Instruction under Governor Harrison Reed, and Reed ran the publication. Much more could have been made of the family's involvement in the state, but Graff never pursued it.

The editors' own 1999 book, *Beechers, Stowes, and Yankee Strangers*, began with research very different from Graff's. It started with the diary of abolitionist John Swaim and journal articles that traced his efforts to attract tourists. Swaim saw tourism as a part of a plan to alter the composition of the state's population and to increase the chances that democracy would be realized. The Swaim diary includes many references to Harrison Reed and a few to Reed's future spouse, Chloe Merrick. As years of research passed, it became clear that Merrick, a First Lady of Florida, was a significant historical figure in her own right. Chloe Merrick served as an educator in schools for freed African Americans in the Civil War, and, seeing the wartime needs of children, she organized and led a multi-racial orphanage in Fernandina, Florida. In the process of our study, we found a statement by a historian in the 1950s claiming that Harrison Reed let his wife design many of the social initiatives of his administration. Given Reed's political problems, this seemed both logical and very likely. Our biographical article about Chloe Merrick Reed led to an examination of Harrison Reed's cabinet. State records included reports by Charles Beecher and his recommendations for the development of schools and colleges in Florida. His recommendations were endorsed by educators for years after Beecher left office. Clearly, Stowe's brother had brought both industry and insight to his service in state government, to the obvious delight of the governor's wife. Without knowing it, we had worked our way from a reformer with a plan to start tourism to his prominent and close friends to the brother of a famous novelist. This approach provided, unexpectedly, a powerful explanation for Harriet Beecher Stowe's fifty-two articles about Florida and the book she derived from seventeen of them. Tourism and new residents could forever change the political and social dynamics of Florida—with the potential of a multiracial coalition dominating the state based upon democracy. Harriet Beecher Stowe was not idling away the winters, but seeking to create a permanent place of freedom in the South. In doing so, she changed history a second time by rapidly increasing tourism to the state. This book advances the theme in *Beechers, Stowes, and Yankee Strangers* by returning to the original and previously uncollected articles that the novelist wrote.

In creating this book, the editors were guided by a simple principle: We wanted to faithfully reproduce the author's exact words. We have done our very best to decipher what these were given the tiny print size and often poor quality of the photographs of the originals (available only in microfilm). We hope the errors are few, but for any incurred inadvertently, we apologize to the reader.

Acknowledgments

The authors wish to thank a wonderful group of people. For years, in our writing and research, we have been encouraged by Ann and Greg Riccardi, as well as by Ann's father, Kent Miller. Even the Riccardis' daughters, Mary, Christina, and Elizabeth, have been an endless source of thoughtful kindness. Our young son once asked, "Are the Riccardis family?" No, but they are the best friends one could ever imagine.

Over the last decade, we stayed involved with Stowe's relationship to Florida by turning to her cousins' and half-sister's lives in the Civil War. This kept us thinking about the novelist and her connections to the state. This could not have happened without the Harriet Beecher Stowe Center and its Collections Manager, Beth Giard Burgess. The Center and Beth Burgess are extraordinary resources.

Four other people were very important—Canter Brown, Jr., and Stan Williams were always a source of encouragement. Roxane Fletcher helped the authors at each step in the creation of this work. She is a wonderful line editor whose advice was invaluable. Many of this work's strengths came from Roxane's talent, wisdom, and insight. At the Florida Historical Society Press, Kirsten Russell brought great skill to preparing the manuscript for publication. To her we owe our warmest thanks.

Changing History Twice

An Introduction by John and Sarah Foster

Tourism in Florida began generations earlier than is generally supposed. The industry predates the Miami of the glamorous 1920s and the palatial hotels of railroad builders of the 1880s and 1890s. In fact it can be traced to the end of the Civil War and a small group of writers in the Jacksonville area. The most notable person among them was an extraordinary woman in any age, Harriet Beecher Stowe.

When Debby Applegate wrote a book about Stowe's brother, Henry Ward Beecher, she gave it the title *The Most Famous Man in America*. Having penned this title, she had to observe that even he did not have his sister's renown. Stowe was, Applegate declared, "the most famous woman in the English speaking world."[1]

Harriet Beecher Stowe's fame rested and continues to rest upon her novel *Uncle Tom's Cabin*. In writing this novel she chose an African American slave as a hero and then traced his life through a series of tribulations. Tom is ultimately beaten to death out of his owner's hatred—that of the infamous Simon Legree. Legree is a horrible character who despises his slave, Tom, for being a decent and honest Christian. For all the novel's shortcomings, Stowe therein captured a fundamental truth about slavery: slavery gave someone who was reprehensible the legal right to maim and kill someone who was blameless.

The novel became a sensation that had far-ranging consequences. For some Yankees who had never seen slavery, its depiction in the novel made the institution unacceptable in any form. For others, including prominent Europeans, it made the idea of aiding the South during the Civil War unthinkable. President Lincoln is supposed to have greeted her with these words on receiving her in the White House, "So you're the little woman who wrote the book that started this great war!" [2] Whether these words were spoken or not, they convey an element of truth. It is not surprising that countless Americans believe *Uncle Tom's Cabin* to be a novel with a singular distinction—

"it changed history." The longtime political editor for *Harper's Weekly*, George William Curtis, wrote that the book "will always be famous not only as the most vivid picture of an extinct evil system, but as one of the most powerful influences in overthrowing it. The light of her genius flashed the monster [slavery] into hideous distinctness, and the country arose to destroy him."[3]

After the Civil War, Stowe turned her attention to Florida and published *Palmetto-Leaves* in 1873. A biographer observed that *Palmetto-Leaves* "became an overnight best seller. When the book first appeared it became immensely popular and greatly stimulated tourist traffic to East Florida."[4] Before its publication Stowe reported "fourteen thousand tourists" in the state in 1872, and a year after its publication she observed that the number had grown to "forty thousand." [5] "People wanted to [see] the promising new Sunshine State and, if possible, also have a look at the famous author and her house." A biographer asserted that Stowe wrote "arguably the most effective and eloquent piece of promotional literature directed at Florida's potential Northern investors at the time."[6]

Few people now are aware of the former popularity of *Palmetto-Leaves,* and even fewer realize that it represented only roughly a third of Stowe's efforts to attract tourists. *Palmetto-Leaves* consisted of seventeen articles published by her in 1872 as well as several other pieces. The novelist wrote thirteen articles about the state, or travel to the state, before that year and twenty-two after the book's publication. By the time she stopped writing about Florida in 1881, the total number of pieces reached above fifty. Some of this material parallels or repeats parts of *Palmetto-Leaves*; much of it does not. Stowe described St. Augustine once, in the original *Palmetto-Leaves*. The ancient city was already a tourist destination in the 1870s and to address this omission in the current volume, we have included an insightful article from the era by a different author. It conveys something of the adventure of the time—an article which also encouraged the preservation of St. Augustine's historic buildings. The newer items include Stowe's visit to Silver Springs by torchlight—we daresay one of the most dramatic and evocative descriptions ever written about Florida.

This work creates a new Stowe Florida book from some of the same sources as the original. The majority of materials in *Palmetto-Leaves* came from the *Christian Union.*[7] The same pattern continues here. In the years following *Palmetto-Leaves*, Stowe also wrote about Florida in other periodicals and sought to protect wildlife. Her efforts occurred in a particular context. To provide it we have included an article published in Florida by Stowe's brother Charles, in which in 1877-78, he fictionally projects the development of modern Florida a century into the future, forecasting vast urban growth. Stowe, during the same time, became alarmed at the destruction of wildlife in Florida and appealed for protection for its birds.

Florida in the 1860s

To understand Stowe's activities it is necessary to describe the state in her day and to link her activities to those of a group of abolitionists. Other people, especially Jacksonville minister John Swaim, had written articles specifically to attract tourists for almost two years when Stowe first arrived in Florida on March 10, 1867. The state then was so dramatically different from today that current residents might not recognize it. The 1870 census counted only some 187,748 residents, making it the least populated state in the region! (It was also the poorest!) In Stowe's era, a person could traverse miles without seeing another human being. Florida was then a vast frontier with small groups of people possessing very different social origins.

The oldest cultural group of Europeans in the state then and now is the Minorcans. Even though they had a Spanish background, they did not come to Florida during Spanish rule. Rather than arriving in the two-hundred-year period that ran from 1565 to 1763, the Minorcans moved to Florida in 1768, in the British period (1763-1783). When a settlement failed at New Smyrna, the Minorcans relocated to St. Augustine and occupied a town that had been abandoned largely by its original citizens.

Being Spanish-speaking Catholics, the Minorcans were very different from the country settlers who drifted into Florida from the backwoods of Georgia—most of whom were descendants of the original English Protestants who settled in the region in the early eighteenth century. These families raised corn, cattle, and hogs in the vast stretches of pine-covered sand that ran for more than a hundred miles, from the interior west of Jacksonville to the red clay hills east of Tallahassee. Because these people used bullwhips to drive their livestock, they became known as "Crackers." The lives of these people have been portrayed in literature, most famously in Marjorie Kinnan Rawlings's novel *The Yearling*.

With little access to schools and churches, the Crackers varied from the planters who settled in the five counties around Tallahassee. Since this region's red clay soil offered the potential of raising cotton, it attracted families from Virginia. A number of them purchased large tracts of land and moved their slaves to this area, replicating the model of society they had known elsewhere. African American slaves formed almost half of the state's population. While the majority resided in Planter or Old South Florida, they also could be found in the Sea Islands north of St. Augustine and in the old city itself. The treatment of slaves also varied, since some residents near the east coast observed Spanish customs, giving slaves some protection. By the 1840s, when Florida was still a territory, it had different and distinct populations—one Hispanic, one frontier or country, and one pursuing the wealth and power of the Old South.

The fourth Florida, or modern Florida, simply did not exist in 1840 or in 1860. The economy of the modern state rests on three elements: tourists, winter residents, and novel agricultural crops—winter vegetables and citrus grown for Northern markets. The famous Florida began to come into existence at the end of the Civil War, at a house in Jacksonville in the spring of 1865. The dwelling was owned by the Northern Methodist minister John Sanford Swaim and his wife Catherine, who were seeking boarders. They also had grander ambitions than renting rooms and serving meals.

Before the Swaims arrived in Jacksonville, abolitionists in the Civil War had already discussed plans for seizing Florida. In 1862, the state's tiny and fragmented population suggested that Federal troops could easily overrun it—an idea that grew in significance in the winter of 1863-64. With the reelection of President Abraham Lincoln on the horizon and General Sherman's march across Georgia many months away, the elimination of a Southern state from the war could have been a political coup. There were a number of factors that added to the plan's feasibility. First, ports and military installations were already occupied by the Union troops on Florida's east coast—at Fernandina and at St. Augustine. From these bases, Federal troops raided the state's interior in 1863. Second, the composition of Florida's population made it even more vulnerable. In the census of 1870, whites outnumbered African Americans by just 4,366 persons; during the war this number would have been smaller. Significant numbers of white Southerners served in Confederate armies far from the state, while a small portion of the white population, especially in ports, were Unionists. Unionists in Florida were often oppressed by Confederates. As a recent writer put it, many "Secessionists demanded unanimity, and vigilantes and Rebel authorities cracked down hard on dissent."[8]

Perhaps the most prominent plan to capture Florida came from Eli Thayer, a well-known abolitionist who had been active in Kansas before the war. In 1862, Thayer suggested that northerners be sent to Florida during the war as settlers. He wanted some "twenty thousand volunteers to establish free-labor farming communities."[9] As part of the plan to aid in their success, Thayer proposed that they would serve as a component of the U.S. Army: as military personnel, they would be supplied by the War Department. Once security had been established, the settlers would leave military service and their families could join them in the interior of Florida. A variation of the Thayer plan would have replaced the northern settlers with freed African Americans—an idea that appealed to Frederick Douglass.[10]

Although the Thayer plan was not implemented, Florida did become the place where black Federal troops were first used in combat. Among the units that eventually saw action in the state was the famous Massachusetts 54th Infantry. The success of these efforts in 1863 created "a new day for the cause of black recruitment. From that time forward the War Department raised black units systematically and aggressively."[11]

Modifying Thayer's Dream for Florida

John Swaim arrived in Florida in the summer of 1864, and within months adapted Thayer's ideas to postwar conditions. The state was still vulnerable, and if African Americans held the franchise, they and the Unionists were a majority in many counties. An influx of Yankees, even in modest numbers, could open the door to dominating Florida politically. John Swaim wrote, "We want to out vote" traditional Southerners "and hold them as a helpless minority." Then he used words from Thayer's heart, "we will settle 'em out. Come Kansas and Nebraska over them."[12]

To attract Yankees to Florida, John Swaim began sending letters and articles to the Newark, New Jersey, newspaper the *Sentinel of Freedom*, which promptly published them and multiplied their effect by also printing them in a subsidiary publication, the *Newark Daily Advertiser*. The first article, from April 12, 1865, stated that the nearby village of Mandarin "furnishes a pretty good supply of oranges for table." Then to lure Yankees, he added that no one "could estimate the quantity of oranges, lemons, bananas, pineapples, and early garden vegetables that might be furnished to our northern market."[13]

In the coming years, from 1865 to July 1869, John Swaim returned to such themes in almost a dozen articles. He repeatedly described exotic agricultural crops and the monies that could be made. In August 1865, he wrote, "The chances for a young man of limited means are better here in Florida than in any [other] portion of the South." Better yet, small colonies of Yankees should come and help "control this 'Italy of America.'"[14] Swaim was subsequently joined in his writing efforts by a son and then by a group of writers who published five or six letters or articles a year. By the end of Reconstruction in 1876, the entire collection in the *Sentinel of Freedom* ran to more than sixty items.[15]

The Florida that these Yankees were to start would be markedly different from that of the past. Swaim envisioned a place of freedom in the South governed by a multiracial coalition—a mixture of African Americans, Unionists, and Yankees. The earlier groups in the state, the Minorcans, the Crackers, and Old South Planters, would just become irrelevant minorities. To realize such a Florida required that Northerners respond to the articles in the *Sentinel of Freedom.* There is evidence that they did respond. By the beginning of 1870 it was claimed that people from New Jersey could be found in every town in Florida in the winter.[16] In 1869, Ledyard Bill wrote a small book, *A Winter in Florida,* which included "Hints to the Tourist." He described Jacksonville as a place transformed. The reason for the change is evident. "On every hand, we behold the magic touch of Northern hands and Northern capital." Bill went on to say, "The population of the place is about six thousand, increased during the winter months to about eight thousand, by the influx of strangers from ... the North." Until the late 1860s, the writer added, "adequate accommodations for this large number" had not existed.[17] Confirming this idea, a different person recalled, "When I came to [Jacksonville] in 1866-67, I think it would have pushed the hotels and boarding houses hard to accommodate a hundred strangers arriving upon any day."[18]

Links between John Swaim and Harriet Beecher Stowe

It is clear that Stowe knew the minister's objectives and pursued them. Southerner Diane Roberts outlined the events: "After the Civil War, a cabal of high-toned Northerners concocted a plan to save Florida's slaveholding soul by colonizing it with progressive New Englanders." By importing "right-thinking settlers, the Yankees and the ex-slaves could outvote anybody." Roberts gives credit for the plan to Swaim, the "master theorist of Florida as a tourist destination."[19] Once he and a few friends implemented their project, they received unexpected support: They "got a public relations boost when an anti-slavery megastar decided to relocate. [She was] the world famous author of *Uncle Tom's Cabin.*"[20]

Knowledge of Swaim's plan came to the novelist several ways. The minister was a close friend of Harrison Reed and his diary for 1866 mentions the soon-to-be governor more than any other resident of

Jacksonville. With a home just a short distance away from Stowe's, Reed had personal contact with the novelist. The "cabal" itself formed after Reed married Chloe Merrick. Keen on influencing educational policy, the new First Lady of Florida needed a person to head the state's public school system. Because Mrs. Reed was a knowledgeable educator, she wanted a man who would not only listen to her but also work closely with her. Charles Beecher had a proven record in this regard and soon found himself in the governor's cabinet. Charles was a favorite brother of the novelist. More than a decade before the Civil War, he had been a source of knowledge about slavery for Stowe when she wrote *Uncle Tom's Cabin*, and then Charles had accompanied her on her tour of Europe after the book's publication.

In forming the cabal, Mrs. Reed was helped by having an extensive knowledge of Stowe's relatives. Historians have long recognized the presence of Stowe's half-brother, James, in Jacksonville during the Civil War, and son Fred in the same area afterwards. What has not been known is the wartime presence in Florida of three women with whom the novelist shared familial bonds. While it is unlikely that Chloe Merrick Reed ever met Stowe's half-sister, Isabella, who came to Jacksonville for a few days in 1864, Chloe knew Stowe's two first cousins. Harriet Ward Foote Hawley and her little sister Kate lived for months in Fernandina when Chloe Merrick taught in the village's schools.[21] The women had much in common: Chloe and Hawley were the same age and shared a strong commitment to abolition. During the war, both women also explored freedom by breaking with traditional roles assigned to their sex. Chloe established an orphanage, raised funds for it in New York, and successfully led it as an administrator. Harriet Hawley, in the same period, garnered public notoriety through writing. She wrote eight newspaper articles about her experiences in the Civil War South, half of them from Florida. There were only seven women known to have served as journalists at that time.[22]

Mandarin and the *Christian Union*

When Stowe came to Florida in 1867, she brought her brother Charles with her. Charles Beecher had spent considerable time in prewar New Orleans and possessed first-hand experience in the South. The novelist also benefited from the knowledge of her sister Isabella and her cousin Harriet Hawley, both of whom would come to live in the same small neighborhood in West Hartford. With so many of Stowe's relatives with recent Florida experience, this for her was no voyage into the unknown.

The often-stated purpose of Stowe's visit to Jacksonville was to check on her son Fred. Fred Stowe had been wounded in the Civil War, and medications only aggravated his alcoholism. By placing him with a few cousins on a rented cotton plantation south of Jacksonville, the novelist minimized the scandal her son could create. But to her dismay, Fred could not manage a farm any better than he could manage himself. Finding the venture failing miserably, Stowe crossed the river to Mandarin and immediately became enraptured with an orange grove. She hated the long New England winters and viewed March snowstorms as nightmares. She immediately ordered funds to purchase an orange grove and then spent every winter in Florida until her husband's health collapsed in 1884. Before the visit Stowe knew that the state offered a paradisiacal alternative to winters she dreaded, and Mandarin with oranges in full bloom proved to be idyllic. Many of the fifty-some articles, letters, and notes she published about Florida, rhapsodized about the beauties and exoticism of the state.

Harriet Beecher Stowe began routinely to write about Florida in 1869 and published articles in *Hearth and Home*. When her famous brother became an editor and owner of the *Christian Union* in 1870, she published there. This weekly newspaper printed Henry Ward Beecher's speeches and sermons, items by his wife Eunice, and theological notes by another brother. To this Stowe added whatever she wished to submit. In late 1877 and much of 1878, the *Christian Union* carried a serial version of Stowe's last novel, *Paganuc People*. In addition the newspaper published book reviews, essays by promi-

The Stowe Residence in Mandarin, Florida: illustration. State Library and Archive of Florida

nent writers, and articles about Biblical topics. In this period Henry Ward Beecher was in one denomination and his sister in another. To solve this problem the *Christian Union* skipped beyond such narrow limits, declaring itself to be "evangelical, independent, and unsectarian." In its advertisements, the periodical claimed lofty goals, "treating all current events with fearless impartiality; in moral and social questions progressive, but not ultra; in religion catholic, but not indifferent." [23]

By writing in the *Christian Union*, Stowe gained a considerable audience. The newspaper claimed 81,000 subscribers in 1872, most of whom were affluent New Yorkers.[24] With such a readership, the newspaper version of *Palmetto-Leaves* may have reached a larger group than the book. The combination of a famous author, Stowe, and a highly popular platform, the *Christian Union*, lends support to the novelist's observation that Florida tourism tripled between 1872 and 1874. There is creditable evidence that this is true.

Evidence of Change

An obvious measure of tourism is the construction and location of hotels. This is just as true today as it was over 130 years ago. The evidence is clear—four hotels were built in Jacksonville, Florida, within a few years of each other. Between 1873 and the end of 1876, the Grand National, Nichols House, the Windsor Hotel, and the Carleton were constructed and opened to the public. They joined two other establishments, the St. Johns and the more important St. James Hotel. The latter began service on January 1, 1869, with "hot and cold baths—an innovation in that day; there were bowling alleys and a billiard room for the amusement of the guests." The St. James Hotel gained two substantial additions, the first being in 1872 and the last in 1881. At the end of these modifications, the hotel had "accommodations for 500 guests."[25] A local historian states that the St. James became "the most famous hotel in the South and for a long time was the Mecca of the wealthy tourist in Florida. Its fame was international; its registers carried the names of the prominent people

The St. James Hotel in Jacksonville, Florida. State Library and Archive of Florida.

of the time from the President of the United States down, with a sprinkling of lesser dignitaries of Europe."[26]

The timing of the hotel construction was extraordinarily high-risk. When experts discussed the economic problems of the United States in 2008 and 2009, they often referred to the Great Depression and to the 1958 recession. On a few occasions economists have mentioned the depression of the 1870s, when the economy unraveled after the noted financier Jay Cooke overspeculated in railroad bonds and declared bankruptcy. A panic followed in September, 1873, and the results were so severe that the New York Stock Exchange closed for ten days! It was believed that 5,000 businesses collapsed by the following fall. The economy recovered somewhat in the middle of the decade, only to convulse again in 1878. During this turmoil the four Jacksonville hotels were opened; nothing but tourism can explain their purpose. Before the Civil War, the city had only two thousand residents, two hotels, and an economy driven largely by sawmills and the timber industry.[27] Of these hotels, one burned in 1859 and the other was destroyed during the war. After the conflict, the town's population tripled to 6,000 residents by 1869. Such phenomenal growth came from tourism, an industry that produced prosperity in

Dining room of the St. James Hotel in Jacksonville, Florida. State Library and Archive of Florida.

the midst of a famous depression: "Jacksonville in the period 1872-1875 was a thriving little city." [28]

A few historians have recognized the period after the Civil War, the Reconstruction, as an important era for tourism. The state's first official librarian, William T. Cash, wrote, "During the Reconstruction there were many northern immigrants, and it was then that the development of Central and South Florida really began." In the next sentence, Cash does link this development to Stowe, but only obliquely. "For several years Mrs. Harriet Beecher Stowe, author of *Uncle Tom's Cabin*, lived in Florida and here wrote a book of impressions."[29] In describing early tourism in St. Augustine, Thomas Graham notes, "Harriet Beecher Stowe penned marvelous stories to magazine readers in the North, describing the magic by which winter could be turned into spring simply by stepping aboard . . . a train to the Land of Flowers." As a consequence, "thousands of perfectly healthy, mostly wealthy people were taking Mrs. Stowe's advice and visiting the state for the sheer pleasure of it."[30]

There is an obvious relationship—a world-famous author wrote articles and published a book about Florida, and then observed a dramatic increase in tourism. The increase had to have been real, even compelling, since investors found the funds to construct hotels in the midst of a famous economic depression. The issue is significant because Harriet Beecher Stowe actually changed history twice. In the second instance, her writing abruptly tripled tourism in Florida, defying the formidable economic conditions of the day.

"Lift Every Voice and Sing"

While both John Swaim and Harriet Beecher Stowe should be remembered for starting and then expanding tourism in Florida, they might individually celebrate a very different consequence of their actions. News of Jacksonville's hotels traveled widely, even to the Bahamas. In 1869 James Johnson left the Royal Victoria in Nassau for the St. James Hotel, where he served as its headwaiter for more than a decade. As his son recalled, "Doubtless the hotel had been planned, and may even have been under construction, before he arrived. The St. James was for many years the most famous and fashionable of all the Florida resort hotels."[31] When the child explored the St. James with his father it was almost beyond belief. As he recalled, "The wide steps, the crowded verandas, the music, the soft, deep carpets of the lobby; this was a world of enchantment." Later, when taken to the dining room, the child saw yet another place of magic. "My father, peerless and imposing in full-dress clothes, strikes a gong and the waiters spring to stations and stand like soldiers at attention; I am struck with wonder at the endless rows of tables now revealed, the glitter of silver, china, and glass, and the array of napkins folded so that they look like many miniature white pyramids."[32]

Mr. Johnson's wife, Helen Louise, joined a church—a northern Methodist one that John Swaim had organized in 1866—where she led the choir for decades. When her mother came to Jacksonville, she joined it too. Ebenezer, as it was called, was important to the Johnson family and their sons joined its congregation when they became adults.[33]

The multiracial world that John Swaim sought was dramatized on two remarkable occasions, both seen by the Johnsons' children. When ex-president Ulysses S. Grant came to Jacksonville in 1880, it was an event. The eldest son recalled, "The crowd at the station was dense and mixed, white and black." After waiting for a long time, the train arrived. As the general walked down the platform to dignitaries, a black woman "darted across the open space straight for General Grant, threw her arms around his neck, gave him a resounding kiss on the cheek, then kneeling down presented him with her bunch of flowers." The woman's action emboldened James Johnson's son James to act. Later at the hotel, as he passed the general with a group of children, he put out his hand and the former president "took it." He later exclaimed, "I had shaken hands with General Grant."[34]

On a very different occasion, the younger James Johnson saw Frederick Douglass speak to a multiracial group in Jacksonville. He remembered watching in awe as the great man "moved a large audience of white and colored people by his supreme eloquence." Then, in a period of questions and answers, someone asked Douglass about having a white wife. He responded honestly, "In my first marriage I paid my compliments to my mother's race; in my second marriage I paid my compliments to the race of my father." [35]

In his autobiography James Weldon Johnson recalled those years when he traveled to Europe and no longer faced the racism he had encountered in adulthood. In France "I recaptured for the first time since childhood the sense of being just a human being."[36] While young he had experienced the dream of freedom sought by John Swaim and Harriet Beecher Stowe as a tangible reality. From the crucible of all these experiences the Johnson children, James Weldon and John Rosamond, would write "Lift Every Voice and Sing," one of the greatest hymns of freedom ever written in America.

Pretending that Harriet Beecher Stowe and *Palmetto-Leaves* Did Not Exist

There are historians and writers who chose to ignore the beginnings of tourism because of their own prejudice. Foremost among these is the local historian, T. Frederick Davis, who published his *History of Jacksonville, Florida, and Vicinity* in 1925. Davis carefully recorded the growth of tourism and the construction of hotels, without ever mentioning who started the tourist industry or why. But there is an explanation for his curious behavior. According to Davis, Jacksonville had "her full quota" of "carpet-baggers" in the Reconstruction. He went on to explain carefully that all Yankees of the period were not "carpet-baggers." The exceptions were "conservative" businessmen who sought "bona-fide residence and legitimate investment." These people tended to be overlooked "in the overwhelming preponderance of political adventurers and fanatics."[36] The son of a Confederate soldier, T. Frederick Davis was not about to mention either Harriet Beecher Stowe or *Palmetto-Leaves*. When Davis described major annual events after Reconstruction, he also chose to ignore Ulysses S. Grant's visit to the city in 1880. Yet the visit of President Grover Cleveland in 1888 received an entire section.Davis tells us that the president received "the most brilliant pageant and parade ever staged here. The presidential train arrived amidst the roar of Wilson's Battery and the party was greeted at the station by cheering thousands, playing bands, and boom of cannon." Later in the evening there was "a grand reception in the parlors of the St. James Hotel. The crowds were so great that the streets were blocked with a mass of people. Mrs. Cleveland's grace and beauty were remarked upon by everyone, and the spontaneous enthusiasm was for her almost as much as for the President himself." [37] Beside such a description, his overt omissions are revealing.

Sadly, Davis is not an isolated case of someone conveniently ignoring the origins of Florida tourism. In more recent times, David Leon Chandler in his biography of Henry Flagler dismissed all of the early developments in tourism. He begins simply by saying that when Flagler came to Florida in 1878, he did not like the hotels in Jacksonville.[39] Without ever exploring what existed at that time or who started tourism, Chandler makes Flagler loom ever more important. The builder of the railroad from Jacksonville to Key West and a series of luxury hotels became, according to Chandler, the "founder" of Florida. While Flagler did make a dramatic contribution to the development of the state, he did not start tourism. The tourists were already coming when the industrialist first came to Florida. He moved them to new locations and to new resorts, investing millions of dollars in the process.

There are also curious omissions in histories of the state, especially in Tebeau and Marina's *A History of Florida.* In a work of some six hundred pages the authors appear to have omitted Stowe and *Palmetto-Leaves.* If they did mention her, she was not worth listing in an index that runs for more than a dozen pages. Tebeau and Marina would not have regarded Stowe as a "fanatic," so she was probably disregarded because she was a woman. Historians of Charlton W. Tebeau's generation seldom gave attention to women, and the lengthy index to his history of the state lists very few. The additional omissions, by the way, include the famous novelists Marjorie Kinnan Rawlings and Zora Neale Hurston, and the distinguished environmentalist Marjory Stoneman Douglas. All these women were far more important than most of the endless cast of males.[40]

The Significance of Florida in Stowe Biographies

The shortcomings of state and local histories have not been recognized by Stowe scholars. By describing the novelist's life in Florida as a private affair, they have created little foundation for response. Stowe's Florida involvement is left as an enigma that few of her biographers have addressed. The beginning of the novelist's life in Mandarin, in fact, coincided with the Lady Byron affair. Stowe knew Lord Byron's wife and had been told by her how she had been abused by the poet. By publishing this information, Stowe was trying to address the plight of women. But this venture into controversy went badly astray. The novelist did not have conclusive proof, leaving herself open to the charge that she had used a tawdry tale for her own profit. If Stowe had written a statement that paralleled John Swaim's published plan for seizing Florida, it could have made her a potential target of the Klan, among other negative consequences. Wisely, she chose to write about the state without explaining her goals. Why risk turning Florida into a violent Kansas when silence could produce a peaceful one? This was in full keeping with Stowe's retreat to "her earlier position of speaking indirectly and attempting to wield her influence behind the scenes." [41]

It is also understandable that biographers would give minor attention to Stowe's Florida experiences—given the novelist's vast published works and a life spanning much of a century. They are unaware that Stowe wrote "Florida's first environmental broadside," "Protect the Birds," and sought legal force to preserve nature. As a result, the novelist's status as an environmentalist has remained unappreciated.[42]

The point of this work is that Stowe's genius is more complex and amazing than even her biographers have realized. While the novelist was aware of the environmental destruction, she still pursued the founding of modern Florida. The new economy was intended to create a place of genuine opportunity: a place where freedom would be fully achieved.

Notes

1. Debby Applegate, *The Most Famous Man in America: The Biography of Henry Ward Beecher* (New York: Doubleday, 2006), 12. The *Florida Times-Union* said Henry Ward Beecher "was the greatest preacher of his generation. He impressed himself indelibly upon his times, and with his death there has passed away from us an unquestionably great man." March 9, 1887.
2. Joan D. Hedrick, *Harriet Beecher Stowe: A Life* (New York: Oxford University Press, 1994), vii.
3. The Curtis letter appeared in an article in the June 15, 1882, *New York Times*. The *Florida Times-Union* said that Harriet Beecher Stowe "produced on the minds of the American people a greater effect than even her distinguished brother Henry Ward Beecher. She did more than any other one person to bring on the war and put an end to slavery." (July 2, 1896)
4. Olav Thulesius, *Harriet Beecher Stowe in Florida, 1867 to 1884* (Jefferson, NC: McFarland & Company, 2001), 94.
5. *Christian Union*, May 5, 1874.
6. Thulesius, Harriet Beecher Stowe, 94.
7. John T. Foster and Sarah Whitmer Foster, *Beechers, Stowes, and Yankee Strangers* (Gainesville, FL: University Press of Florida), 93.
8. Stephen V. Ash, *Firebrand of Liberty: The Story of Two Black Regiments that Changed the Course of the Civil War* (New York: W. W. Norton, 2008), 77.
9. Ibid., 78.
10. Ibid., 79.
11. Ibid., 202.
12. *Sentinel of Freedom*, September 29, 1868.
13. Ibid., April 25, 1865.
14. *Newark Daily Advertiser*, August 29, 1865.
15. Foster and Foster, *Beechers, Stowes, and Yankee Strangers,* 125.
16. *Sentinel of Freedom*, February 9, 1870.
17. Ledyard Bill, *A Winter in Florida* (New York: Wood and Holbrook, 1869), 82.
18. *Semi-Tropical*, January 1876.
19. Diane Roberts, *Dream State: Eight Generations of Swamp Lawyers, Conquistadors, Confederate Daughters, Banana Republicans, and Other Florida Wildlife* (Gainesville, FL: University Press of Florida), 135.
20. Ibid.
21. Foster and Foster, "Historic Notes and Documents: Harriet Ward Foote Hawley: Civil War Journalist," *Florida Historical Quarterly*, Spring 2005, 448-67.
22. See J. Cutler Andrews' *The North Reports the Civil War* and his *South Reports the Civil War*.
23. *Christian Union*, January 9, 1878.

24. Ibid., 1872.
25. T. Frederick Davis, *The History of Jacksonville and Vicinity*, (Jacksonville, FL: Jacksonville Historical Society, 1925), 487.
26. Ibid., 488.
27. Ibid., 95; A writer in the 1870s states that "Jacksonville, before war" had "twenty-one first class sawmills." *Semi-Tropical*, November 1876.
28. Davis, *The History of Jacksonville*, 153.
29. William T. Cash, *Story of Florida* (New York: American Historical Society, 1938), 484.
30. Thomas Graham, *The Awakening of St. Augustine: The Anderson Family and the Oldest City* (St. Augustine: St. Augustine Historical Society, 1978), 167.
31. James Weldon Johnson, *Along this Way: The Autobiography* (New York: Da Capo Press, 2000), 15.
32. Ibid., 16.
33. Ibid., 10.
34. Ibid., 43.
35. Ibid., 61.
36. Ibid., 209.
37. Davis, *History of Jacksonville*, 147-48.
38. Ibid., 177-78.
39. David Leon Chandler, *Henry Flagler, The Astonishing Life and Times of the Visionary Robber Baron Who Founded Florida* (New York: Macmillan, 1986), 87. Chandler describes the hotels in Jacksonville as "primitive." If Flagler didn't like his accommodations in the city, he should have moved to the St. James.
40. Charlton W. Tebeau and William Marina, *A History of Florida* (Coral Gables: University of Miami Press, 1999). Tebeau and Marina did spend, however, a number of paragraphs discussing the administration of Governor Fred P. Cone; see pages 391-92. Cone is normally remembered for obstructing anything that would have ameliorated the effects of the Great Depression.
41. Accounts of the Lady Byron affair can be found in Joan Hedrick's biography of Stowe on pages 353-370. The quotation is from page 370.
42. Even Joan Hedrick's biography does not mention "Protect the Birds." While Hedrick identified over twenty topics in her index upon which Stowe had "views," including abolition and the Beecher-Tilton scandal, the environment is not a part of the list. Michael Grunwald in *The Swamp* labeled "Protect the Birds" as "Florida's first environmental broadside," page 119.

Silver Springs by Torchlight

Stowe wrote this article after her evocative journey to Silver Springs.[1] *Although the novelist had known about the springs she had intentionally avoided visiting them for years. The hesitation came from the dubious appearance of the steamboat used for the trip. To reach the springs required running up the small river, the Ocklawaha, which carries water that flows from the spring. The Ocklawaha meandered through a combination of swamps, glens, and forests. With trees projecting into the river's narrow course, a typical steamboat of the period would have been damaged quickly. The craft used for the journey had to be small and narrow, with few windows. When Stowe first saw the steamboat late one afternoon she had an immediate, negative reaction; it looked like a "coffin in twilight."*[2]

We have done it! Whether in the body or out, we have been to dream-land, to the land of the fays and the elves, the land where reality ceases and romance begins.[3] In the measurement of earth, and in the geographic language of reality this was accomplished in a six days' journey, on the little steamer *Okalawaha*.[4] We left Mandarin at eleven o'clock on Thursday, March 27, and returned to it again the next Tuesday afternoon. We had often noticed, passing by on the river, the little steamer *Okalawaha*, looking for all the world like a gray square cotton [bale?], and we confess that we shuddered at the idea of going on a bush-whacking tour through the native swamps of the alligator in such a suspicious looking craft as that.

But the experiences of more venturesome friends, who dared and did—went up and came back with songs of joy upon their head—persuaded us. Our tourist friends, persons of renowned good sense, came back from their trip fairly inebriated with enthusiasm, wild with incoherent raptures. They had seen Europe and Italy, Naples and the blue grotto, but never, never had they in their lives seen aught so entrancing as this.[5] It was a spectacle, weird, wondrous, magical—to be remembered as one of the things of a lifetime.

Well, really, after this who would not expect to be disappointed? Who, going with such a fanfaronade of ex [text missing] would not come on back a little worse for experience?[6] Nevertheless we have been, and come back, and are not disappointed, but prepared to chorus the most extravagant laudations of our friends. How it is we know not. You know it is a wide-attested fact that there are places and regions on earth where the fays and the dryads, and other wood spirits still live, who enchant the eyes of the comer and bear him off into magical regions, and bewilder him till he don't know whether he has been on earth or under it. We have almost forgotten our classical literature, but we dimly remember the Cave of Trophonius and the shades of the Delphic Oracle, and Lake Avernus, whence Virgil descended into the Elysian Fields.[7] The fountain of immortal youth, which Ponce de Leon supposed was to be found in the heart of Florida, could have been no other than the Silver Spring, whose magical waters, like a great glancing chrysolite, lie in the heart of these unknown forests.[8]

So, while you, my poor, dear, virtuous friends were fighting with roaring March winds up in the "still vexed" North, behold us stepping on board the little steamer *Okalawaha* on a bright day, with a gay and festive party of young people. To begin with our boat was an agreeable disappointment. We had always dreaded the boat as the abatement of the pleasure; for what, we said, could be done with twenty passengers on such a little craft? We found, however, a neat, well-ventilated cabin, with berths for eight ladies, as comfortable as could be desired. Then there were six more state-rooms, opening from the central cabin, of two berths each. The captain was all accommodation; every hand on board, cook, steward, waiter were as good-natured and obliging as could be desired, and the passengers, in return, were good-natured; polite to each other, and unexacting in their requirements; and so the little bark came to be looked on as quite a nice little home. As to our table, it was crowded, to be sure,

The steam ship *Ocklawaha*. State Library and Archive of Florida.

both with dishes and with guests; and as the whole cookery had to be done in a place no bigger than a good-sized pocket handkerchief, the results were certainly not to be severely criticized. If the proof of the pudding be in the eating, certainly the guests did ample justice to their meals, eating to right and left in a most complimentary manner. In fact, although we started on this expedition feeling rather poorly, and with a very faint appetite, we became uncritical devourers of whatever was set before us, merely from living all day in the fine open air that blew across the boat's deck.

Our voyage circumstantially may be thus narrated:

From the pier in Mandarin, as aforementioned, we stepped aboard, about eleven o'clock in the forenoon of Thursday. Our little slow stern-wheel boat made the best of her way upward and reached Palatka just about seven o'clock.[9] The boat lay there an hour or two, then we all took to our berths, opened our little slides of windows for the river breeze to blow through, and resigned ourselves peacefully to sleep. In the middle of the night we were waked by the scraping of branches against our little boat, and looked dreamily out to see that we were gliding through palmetto forests and weird grottos, lit up with blazing pine torches. It seemed part of a fantastic dream as our weary eyes closed and the boat rippled on.

Friday morning we were waked by the singing of birds in the branches, to find ourselves still gliding through the arches of an unbroken forest. We sat on a little platform in front of the pilot-house, and glided along, seeing into the very heart of the tropical mysteries.

Sometimes the whole way seemed given up to palmetto groves—rising in every conceivable shape and variety—growing with a luxuriance and a grace indescribable. The trunk of the palms sometimes seems a regular and exact pillar of basket-work, built up twenty or thirty feet. In the crevices of the basket-work large ferns and air plants take root, so that the tree is often a pillar of various foliage and flowers.

Here and there the palms lean aslant over the water; they throw themselves forward and meet in arches overhead; they lie creeping in scaly folds on the ground; they wave sixty or seventy feet high in the air. The oldest palms have shed the scaly basket-like enclosure, and are round and smooth like columns, the latest scales only remaining high up in the air, and the ferns and vines waving from them like streamers. But by far the greater part of the way, the palmetto was gracefully intermixed with other trees. The cypress, with its glistening white trunk and shapely pillars, rises to an immense height: its snowy columns reflected far down in the smooth glassy water. The palms sometimes seemed embraced in the white arms of cypress, leaning their plumy heads against its branches, their dusky hue contrasting with the vivid yellow green of the cypress feathers. The other trees were the water-ash, the loblolly bay, the magnolia glauca, certain varieties of red maple and water-oaks, and a few of the magnolia grandiflora.[10] Growth seemed to have run riot here, to have broken into strange goblin forms, such as Doré might have chosen for his weird imaginings.[11] Here, where foraged nature has been let alone, where the fiery heats and the moist soil have conspired together, there is a netting and convoluting, a twisting and weaving and intertwining of all sorts of growths; and one might fancy it an enchanted forest, where the trees were going to change into something new and unheard of.

The alligator seems to belong most naturally in these shades. The long-necked water-turkey sits perched gravely on the boughs overhead, or dives in the waters below.[12] The limpkin, with its long neck and legs and its wild plaintive cry, the white crane and blue crane, the pink and white curlew, these seem the fit inhabitants for whom these forest solitudes are made.[13] The dreamy wildness, the perfect strangeness of all this, its utter unlikeness to anything one has ever seen, inclines one to aimless reverie. The stories of Tick and Touquet seem quite possible here.[14]

The boat glides on, from hour to hour, as the river winds and turns, and doubles upon itself, with still the same flowery solitudes reverberating with the same wild cries of birds, glittering with slanting sunbeams festooned with waving garlands that hang from tree to tree.

At intervals the steam-whistle startles the birds and makes the forest echoes ring—it is a sign that we are coming to a landing.

The inhabited country of this region is an elevated tract that lies back of the river, and these landings are breathing holes; vistas opening from the interminable forest mystery into human abodes. Generally at one of these landings a letter-box is nailed up conspicuously on the trunk of some cypress or other large tree, where letters and papers are left for the families whose invisible homes lie beyond.

Sometimes a group of two or three smart hunters in high peaked hats, attired in homespun garments with knives in their boots, stand leaning on their guns waiting the approach of the boat.[15] They seemed a grave, taciturn, unsmiling race, long-haired, bearded, and roughly attired; with the shallow complexion and dark eyes that gave intimations of Minorcan blood. They reminded us of the shepherds of the Campania.[16] Occasionally a wild turkey or a saddle of venison hung in the tree, promised a supply to the provision market of the boat. They brought pailfuls of new laid eggs and sometimes baskets of great golden oranges which the captain bought and dispensed liberally among the passengers. The weekly touching of the boats at the lonely landings are the only communication these settlers hold with the outside world. A more solitary life cannot be imagined.

Perhaps our voyage through these unbroken forests might have been in time, somewhat monotonous, had not a dozen or two of mighty hunters kept us from going to sleep by the briskness of their firing. There were on board a few good marksmen, who knew how to hit what they fired at, but almost an equal number of inexperienced hands, foaming at the mouth with excitement and quite likely to hit any one of us as the alligators. The cry, "Dar's a gator," was a signal for a perfect fusillade, much more dangerous to us than to the alligators, who generally dove and paddled off.

The first day on board was a hot one, and was like a Fourth of July in a city, an unintermitted blaze and fizz. Every lady on board had a headache and the coming on of night was a welcome relief. Then came the lighting of the great pine knot brazier over the pilot-house, and we sat on deck watching the weird effects of the fire-light up the long watery aisles and colonnades of the palmy woods. Saturday morning we woke in the broad Savannahs. Waving fields of water-plants, water-lilies, yellow and white arrow-heads, pickerel weed, water-lettuce, and every other aquatic plant that can be thought of, were here in wide sweeping fields of undulating waves.[17] It was a lake of lilies: tall bulrushes, six or seven feet high, waved and nodded, and on every bulrush perched a red-winged blackbird. It was a prairie of birds—they rose in clouds. They sung and capered, lit on the top end of the bulrushes, and slid down to the middle then swung busily with their short airy whistle, the picture of joy. A beautiful little water bird, with blue feathers and red head and feet, flitted over the water-lily leaves, and one or two flocks of green and gold parquets rose on wing and soared away.[18]

The water-turkey and the blue and white crane by their heedless conduct in perching squarely in sight of the boat, destroyed a great deal of our pleasure. We did not want to see them fall, mangled and fluttering, under the awkward shots of some of our sportsmen, and left to starve to death lingeringly, as the boat glided on.

The destructive instincts of the hunter seem to destroy all sympathy with nature, all sense of beauty of scenery, or interest in its various sources of knowledge.

The Savannahs, in which we sailed all day Saturday, gradually merge into a chain of beautiful lakes—Lakes Griffin, Eustace [Eustis] and Harris.[19] We entered Lake Griffin on Saturday evening. It is a charming sheet of water, with high banks, on some of which are fine building sites. In the dim gray of the dawn, Sunday morning, we woke to find ourselves tied up to a wharf at Okahumke [Okahumpka].[20] We turned over and went to sleep, and when we woke again the boat was far on her homeward way again. We were just passing out of Lake Eustace into Lake Griffin [retracing the journey through the lakes] as we left the breakfast table. It was as lovely a day as heart could imagine, angelically clear and fresh, and our quartette sat on the deck and sang hymns in infinite variety.

In our youth a religious hymn was the most long-drawn and doleful sound conceivable. Now, under the genial culture of the Sunday-school, hymns have budded and blossomed; they are full of life, and color and motion.

Sunday night the wonders of our voyage came to a climax. The captain announced to us that the boat would enter the Silver Spring between one and two o'clock, and advised us to sit up if we wanted to see the very finest part of the route.

We did sit up, prepared as we were by a night's experience in wild forest traveling. We were taken by surprise by the wonderful scenes through which we passed.

We seemed floating through an immense cathedral whose white marble columns met in vast arches overhead and were reflected in the glassy depths below. The dusky plumes of the palmetto waving above, lit by torch-light, looked like the fine tracery of a wondrous sculptured roof. The brilliant under-white of the bay leaves, the transparent red of the water maple, and the soft vivid feathers of the cypress, had a magical brilliancy as our light passed through the wooded aisles. The reflected fire-light gave the most peculiar effect. Every trunk, and limb, and branch of the trees, down to the minutest spray, was of glistening whiteness, like ivory. The gray moss that streamed down seemed like craped veils of silver, and was of a wonderful profusion, in some cases veiling the trees entirely.

In the stillness of the night our gliding boat seemed to float like a specter; clouds of fragrance were wafted to us from distant orange groves. The cranes and herons and wild wood birds would wake, dazed with the glare of our torches, and flutter into our very hands as we passed.

We took the one step from the sentimental to the ludicrous, when one of our party most unexpectedly captured a water-turkey from a bough just over our head, and held him aloft in wild excitement. The poor bird made the best use of his long, snaky neck, throwing himself, with open mouth, hither and thither among the company, with a plucky show of fight, till, between laughing and alarm, we were thoroughly discomposed and prevailed on his captor to throw him back into the trees.

What a night was that! Everybody watched and wondered and the most prosaic grew poetic. About one o'clock we glided into the Silver Spring run, and by two, we were all gathered on the lower deck, looking down into transparent depths that gave the impression that our boat was moving through air. Every pebble and aquatic plant we glided over seemed, in the torch-light, invested with prismatic brightness. When the boat at last came to landing in the Silver Spring, we laid us down to sleep, fairly tired out with excitement, to wait for morning.

Monday morning broke bright and beautiful, and there we lay in a little wooded basin a quarter of a mile in diameter, with all the underworld clearly revealed from its translucent depths. The water had the crystalline clearness and the magical prismatic reflections which give such charm to the blue grotto at Capri. Ribs of limestone rock are seen far down, and the spring boils and bubbles upward, throwing up thousands of gallons a minute without making more than a ripple on the surface.

A party of us got into a little skiff and floated over the transparent depth. Every variety of water plant was growing and waving over the varied surfaces of the bottom, which had its heights and depths, its caverns and grottos. We could see the fish darting hither and thither, and mark on the brilliant sands at the bottom various objects which had been thrown in by experimenting travelers. The water was of about the same high temperature with the spring at Green Cave.[21] The shores were clothed with tropical forests all around, and here and there we could see starry flocks of a peculiar and beautiful white lily which grows abundantly on these waters. From a star-shaped calyx of six narrow white leaves comes out a silver cup, from the edges of this cup rise six stamens with their golden heads.[22]

By about ten o'clock we had left the Silver Spring with its crystal waters behind—our romance was over and our faces set homeward. Yet that evening, as we sat on deck going through the narrows of the Okalawaha we felt that the spell of the illusion was not quite broken. The quartette had sung themselves hoarse, and the negro firemen and hands now came forward, and in the shadows of the lower part of the boat, made the woods ring with their strange, wild choruses. They sung through the book of Revelation with the chorus "I John saw," which came in as regularly as a drum-beat, thus:

> Michael fought the dragon,
> I John saw;
> Nine days the battle lasted,
> I John saw.

Dey throwed him out o' heaven,
Dey locked him in a dungeon.
Dey carried the key to Jesus.
Dey laid it on the altar,
I John saw.

The triumphal tramp and swing and force of the chorus gathers from verse to verse, for the negro, instead of tiring as he sings, becomes fired and excited—every fiber of his body quivers in time—and had the boat given room they would have moved in rhythmic dance to their music.

Then there was another solemn and grave air that they called "De White Horse," founded on the passage in Revelations [*sic*] where it is said: "I saw heaven opened, and behold a white horse, and he that sat on him was called Faithful and True; in righteousness doth he judge and make war. And the armies of heaven followed him upon white horses, clothed in white linen, pure and clean."

The song was in "the Dorian mood [mode]," slow and grand, "breathing deliberate valor." It was the call for soldiers for the last battle. [23] It was no dress parade:[24]

It is no call for empty show,
Nor pomp of heraldry;
He calls for valiant soldiers,
Who're not afeared to die.

There was something thrilling and grand in these wild words, breathed into the dark arches of the forest by these weird voices, singing as many parts as the birds and the winds, and all with the same wild accord. And these black men had shown on many a field that they were "not afeared to die."

Then came,
We'll camp a while in de wilderness,
And den we'll all go home.

As the boat passed from the shadows of the Okalawaha to the broad St. Johns, three cheers made the woods ring, and our "camping in the wilderness" was over.

Notes

1. The article originally appeared in the *Christian Union* on May 14, 1873, as "Up the Okalawaha—A Sail Into Fairy-Land."
2. Stowe, *Palmetto-Leaves*, 262.
3. Fays: fairies; dryads: wood nymphs.
4. Stowe's spelling of the river (and the "little steamer" named after it), of course, varies from the modern Ocklawaha.
5. Blue Grotto: a famous location on the north shore of the Isle of Capri.
6. Fanfaronade: bluster or bravado.
7. Cave of Trophonius: one of the most celebrated oracles of ancient Greece. Lake Avernus: a crater in Italy believed by Virgil to be the entrance to the underworld.
8. Chrysolite: olivine or the gem peridot.
9. Palatka: this town was both a tourist center and a transportation hub for interior of the state. In the last third of the nineteenth century Palatka was served by seven steamboat lines and as many as five railroads. It had a population of 1,616 in 1880.
10. Loblolly bay: a small evergreen that has white flowers; magnolia glauca: the small magnolia has the most extensive range of all magnolias in the southeastern US; magnolia grandifloria: southern magnolia famous for its waxy green leaves and large white flowers.
11. Paul Gustave Doré was an illustrator of Poe's "Raven."
12. Water-turkey: anhinga. These darters have snakelike necks. Having fished, their feathers become waterlogged, requiring a period of drying in the sun.
13. Limpkin: a type of wading bird with a long, curved beak. A limpkin looks like an ibis, but with white streaks and splotches; white and pink curlews: a type of sandpiper which has a red color in breeding season.
14. Tick and Touquet: not identified.
15. Hunters with high peaked hats: a description of Florida Crackers.
16. Campania: the region around Naples, Italy.
17. Yellow and red arrow heads: a short aquatic plant with arrow shaped leaves, flowers, and a milky sap; pickerel weed: an aquatic perennial with blue or lavender flowers.
18. Green and gold parquets: the Carolina Parakeet was green with yellow and red heads. Tragically, these birds became extinct in 1918.
19. Lakes Griffin, Eustace [Eustis], and Harris: three lakes to west and north of Leesburg, Florida. In 1891, Charles Norton listed their sizes: Harris at 28 square miles, Griffin at 15 square miles, and Eustis at 13. All of them are miles below Silver Springs on the headwaters of Ocklawaha River.
20. Okahumke [Okahumpka] was a small landing not far from the current turnpike, northwest of Orlando.
21. Green Cave: a famous cave at Capri, Italy.
22. Star-shaped calyx: green projections just below the petals of flowers.

23. Dorian Mood: refers to early church music that had a pattern of whole tones followed by a half tone. See "Dorian Mode" in *The New Grove Dictionary of Music and Musicians,* second edition, edited by Stanley Sadie and John Tyrell, 2001.
24. No dress parade: Stowe knew from both the newspapers and from her half-brother, James C. Beecher, that black soldiers were very formidable in combat.

Travel to Florida

The first tourists in Florida arrived by steam-powered craft from either South Carolina or Georgia. There were very few other options. Before the Civil War most Southern railroads were short, running from major ports into the rural interior without interconnections to other states. With capital limited it took years to repair the damage from the conflict and then to weave a series of small lines into regional rail systems. In January 1874, Stowe carefully described both the maritime choices as well as her first all-rail journey to Florida. This article signals that railroads are fully competitive.[1]

This is about the time that we get from one to two letters a week, and the burden of these letters is pretty much the same. How can we get to Florida? What is the best place? When can we go?

We propose to devote a letter to answering these questions, with the best light our own observation and experience afford. There are two ways of going to Florida, which may be divided in good Geographic fashion, thus:

First, Land; second, Water.

The starting-point, in either case, is New York. New York, you will observe, is getting more and more to be a sort of center of the world, so that if you want to turn up anywhere on the globe, whether in Spain, Italy, Kamschatka [Kamchatka] or China, the first step is to go to New York. Well, then, in New York, you buy a ticket, which, for twenty-seven dollars and a little over, puts you down, safe and sound, in Florida, with only one change—from steamer to steamer at Savannah or Charleston, according to the line. If a person is a fair sailor this route is to be chosen by all means. It is the most convenient, neat and expeditious mode of making the transfer. Moreover, at this same New York [office] you can buy your ticket, if you so desire, not merely to Jacksonville but to any of the points on the St. Johns River, where [there] are boarding houses and hotels. You can go from New York to Magnolia, or Pilatka [Palatka], or Green Cove Springs, or Enterprise equally well with but one change of boat.[2] For ladies traveling alone, for invalids who feel the worry and care of frequent transfers, and for those encumbered with much baggage, this is undoubtedly the safest and most convenient arrangement of the whole affair.

There are two lines of steamers starting from New York which undertake this transfer—the Charleston and the Savannah boats. In the one case the transfer is made at Charleston, and in the other at Savannah, and the two lines are equally good, and connect with the same Florida boats, and either Charleston or Savannah is a fine point to rest at on one's way down.

The steamers do not always connect immediately. There is an interval generally of a day and a night at these intermediate points, where there are fine, well-kept, comfortable hotels, in which one gets a little rest from sea voyaging, and gets heart to finish. The only care is to see one's baggage re-checked at these places for whatever point in Florida one desires to reach. The clerk of the boat is generally most obliging in taking all this care for ladies traveling without protection. The same Florida boats touch both at Charleston and Savannah, so that the further passage can equally well be secured at either point. The average voyage from New York to Charleston is two days and to Savannah three.

At Savannah, the traveler who is uneasy at sea can have the alternative of another boat, which starts at ten o'clock on Wednesday mornings, and instead of going out to the open sea, sails placidly through that inner passage which winds in and out through the belt of Sea Islands, whence in olden time came the famous Sea Island Cotton. The boat is in all respects well kept and comfortable, and the voyage has many peculiar and beautiful points, and, for those who wish to see as much of characteristic Southern scenery as possible, is not to be neglected. Then there is no possibility of sea-sickness, as the voyage is smooth as on a canal boat. You go winding curiously through green islands, sometimes so near that you can catch at the bushes on the shore, and sometimes you stop for an hour or two, when you can go on shore for a walk.

At last, a run of an hour and a half out over open sea brings you to the mouth of the St. Johns River, and certainly there is no one point of view in the Southern land more grand and imposing than this.[3] Never shall we forget the first sight as it broke on us. We lay off in our little steamboat, enveloped in a dense mist, waiting for the fog to

A steamer bringing Northerners to Florida. State Library and Archive of Florida.

rise that we might see our way in. The passage into the river is a narrow and dangerous one, beset with sand-bars and breakers, and it is necessary to be able to see plainly the buoys that mark the channel. Presto! like a curtain rising in the theatre, up went the fog, rolling off in white smoke wreaths, the sun shone out on the blue river and the white foam-caps of the breakers as we sailed triumphantly in. The shores are of white sparkling sand, like new-fallen snow, and from them rise feathery groups of palmettos and dusky live oaks. Flocks of white pelicans stand in ranks on the sand-bars, watching their prey in the boiling waters. The St. Johns is the triumphal entrance into Florida, and it is no wonder that the first explorers who came in at that radiant gate were dazzled and bewildered and gave the river all sorts of poetic names.[4]

Henceforth, the passenger is free of [in] Florida. He has only to abide, and wake, and sleep, and live in his floating house and one by one all its haunts and places of abode will pass before him where to choose. A few hours brings him to Jacksonville, and for those who prefer to live in a city, with the comforts and conveniences which a city can afford, Jacksonville is a very pretty point of rest. There is a great deal of life and motion there—communication with the North is frequent and easy, and with Jacksonville as a base of supply, it is easy to command all the rest of Florida by excursions. The hotels of Jacksonville give every comfort that one may need, and every year the proprietors study new means of making them agreeable. Besides this, Jacksonville is full of private boarding houses, so that, with a little inquiry, places may be found adapted to the means of those who cannot afford hotel life.

Next to Jacksonville, on the west side of the river and within two hours' sail, are three very desirable winter locations. Hibernia is a very charming boarding place, where the inmates have home-like and comfortable surroundings, and something of the domesticity for which one longs in a strange land.[5]

Magnolia, a little further south, has a large and finely-kept boarding house, with several out-cottages and delightful surroundings;[6] and half a mile from that, the little village of Green Cove Springs has two or three hotels and a number of small boarding houses. This place is especially to be recommended for such invalids as suffer from complaints of a rheumatic nature. The large and delightful warm sulphur spring there is a means of restoration of health and comfort that cannot be too highly valued. People of modest means can find private board on reasonable terms at Green Cove.

Still further up the river is the landing of Tecoi [Tocoi] where one takes the [rail] cars for St. Augustine.[7] A ride of fifteen miles puts that quaint old city, with its hotels and boarding houses, its mild, bracing sea air, at the choice of the tourist. Still further south on the river, Pilatka, and farthest of all, Enterprise, have hotels where tourists may find comfortable living. The St. Johns River is the highway, the great water road to the whole—and once upon it you must choose for yourself where to pitch your tent.

Now, a word as to those who cannot come by sea. There are sold at New York railroad tickets which engage to take the buyers through from New York to Florida. They are more expensive than the sea route in the beginning, and then your board during the journey is an additional charge. The whole extra expense is a full one-third more than the route we have described, but as there are those who cannot travel by sea we shall say a friendly word about these. We have just come over one of these routes—the new airline road[8] through Baltimore, Washington, Richmond, Greensboro, Augusta to Savannah, and from Savannah to Jacksonville. We can speak well of this route. The [rail] cars are good, all the officials careful, friendly, and obliging, and the night [sleeping] cars are peculiarly good. Of course, a delicate person cannot perform this whole route without occasional stop for a night to rest, for not withstanding the goodness of the cars and sleeping accommodations, such incessant vibratory motion tells on the brain and nervous system.[9] But the route gives a choice of desirable places to stop. Two or three days at Washington can never come amiss, and a day can be profitably spent at Richmond, especially if you visit the excellent schools for colored people;[10] and the route passes farther through large cities where good accommodations can be found.

A well-filled luncheon-basket, with crackers, potted ham and tongue, pickles and fruit, should by all means be provided in the outset, and at every stopping place you will be able to reinforce this standing fortress with some slight additions. Our longest ride on this road without stopping was from Washington to Savannah, which we accomplished in forty-two hours.[11] At all eligible points we found negro mammies selling fair hot coffee, with tea-cups, sugar, and cream quite handy, and with occasional portions of fried chicken.[12] We found all the officials most polite and attentive, seeing most carefully after unprotected females wherever changes were to be made; and the night berths were a great deal better and easier than any we ever slept in on a steamboat. Nevertheless, glad were we when the quiet, homelike doors of the Pulaski House in Savannah received us and gave us a chance for rest.[13] The Pulaski House, without being showy or pretentious, is peculiarly quiet, homelike, and comfortable. Everything that careful attendance and the best kept table and neatest ordered rooms can do to restore and compose the nerves of a worn out traveler is here done. In fact, the hotels of Savannah are so restful and so healing to the nerves that we do not wonder that Southern travelers often give a week to composing themselves here before taking the last step into Florida. From Savannah there is only a night ride, with good sleeping accommodations, and you awake to breakfast in Jacksonville.[14]

Thus, dear pilgrim inquiring, is your route made out either way, and, in closing, I say that the sunshine, the flowers, the birds, the orange-groves, are all calling to you. Come!

Notes

1. This article originally appeared as "Bird Flights Southward," *Christian Union*, January 21, 1874.
2. Pilatka [Palatka]: this town was both a tourist center and a transportation hub for the interior of the state. In the last third of the nineteenth century Palatka was once served by seven steamboat lines and as many as five railroads; Green Cove Springs was a small yet significant resort a short distance south of Jacksonville. It is described in length in chapter seven. Enterprise: a small community in Volusia County—one of the most southern landings made by nineteenth century steamboats.
3. The original entrance to the St. Johns River was some two miles in width and the channel shifted unpredictably across this opening. It is not surprising

that public pressure was brought on the federal government to reduce the hazards. Construction on jetties began in December, 1880. Davis, 307.

4. The French in the sixteenth century gave the St. Johns River the name "May" since they arrived in its entrance on May 1, 1562. Davis, 37.
5. Hibernia: a tiny community near Green Cove Springs which, at times, had its own identity. It lost its post office in 1931.
6. Magnolia: location of a hotel several miles from Green Cove Springs.
7. Tecoi [Tocoi] was described by Stowe as a "shed and sand-bank, and a little shanty … for refreshments." Tourists waited there for trains to St. Augustine.
8. New air line road: Seaboard Air Line Railroad.
9. This sensitivity may be directly related to Stowe's medical past. Stowe showed evidence of mercury poisoning in the 1840s. Mercury was a major component of calomel, a commonly prescribed nineteenth century medicine.
10. Schools in Richmond: probably refers to the Richmond Colored Normal School, a forerunner of Armstrong High School, or to Wayland Seminary, a forerunner of Virginia Union University.
11. A distance of 524 miles between Washington, DC, and Savannah was covered in forty-two hours.
12. Negro mammies: a generic title for older African American women reflecting the idioms of the time. The reader should remember that Mark Twain used the "N" word in *Huckleberry Finn* (1884) even though Twain was sympathetic to black people.
13. Pulaski House: the Pulaski House to which Stowe refers is not the current establishment in Savannah, but another.
14. Night ride: with a distance of about 120 miles between Savannah and Jacksonville, this suggests a speed of 15 miles an hour.

Before Palmetto-Leaves: A Sermon from Florida

When Stowe spent winters in Mandarin she was often busy. Not for her was today's stereotype of "wintering" in Florida for rest and relaxation or retiring to a life of repose. Her father was a nationally known minister, Lyman Beecher, and she had seven brothers, all of whom served in the ministry. (This does not mean that her brothers took up their father's profession with enthusiasm. Brother Charles fled to antebellum New Orleans and James drifted as far away as China.) Had it not been for the values of the day, Harriet also would have pursued a role in the pulpit. It should be remembered, too, that Stowe's own writings about Mandarin and its surroundings had a calculated purpose. She, like John Swaim, wanted a place of freedom in the South based upon democracy.[1]

This stands in vivid contrast with a current trend observed by the late William R. Maples.[2] *A longtime University of Florida-based forensic anthropologist, Maples knew about countless suicides among elderly retirees. They are often people who retire to the Sunshine State and never become involved. As years pass, spouses die and so do their neighbors. The remaining spouses find themselves a thousand miles or more from family or old friends in New York or New Jersey. In poor health and depressed, these isolated people turn to alcohol or pre-*

scription drugs or suicide. Rather than being a place of happiness, Florida can be a place of desolation.

That was not the path of Stowe. Her efforts and those of her family led to the creation of an Episcopal church in Mandarin in 1883. In this article she seeks to find a modern equivalent of the apostle Paul for the Florida wilderness near her home.[3]

How was the Gospel first made to prevail? It was one of the most improbable, unlikely things to prevail that ever was heard of.

We are so accustomed to looking at the Gospel as it is now in all its respectability, in all of the pomp of rank and wealth, when churches are splendid and crowded, when well dressed people are seen bowing, like grain in the wheat fields, at the name of Jesus, that it will take a stretch of imagination to carry us back to the real situation as it was in the beginning.

How did it look in the small talk of Jew and Greek in the outset?

A little pestilent, obstinate, troublesome tribe of people on the east end of the Mediterranean, who were always in some fracas with their Roman governor, had just got up a mob about a so-called prophet and wonder-worker of their own tribe named Jesus—by all accounts a good man, and one that ought to have been let alone—but the Jews were so very troublesome that Pilate had to give him up to keep the peace. After all, he was only a Jew, and if killing him would settle their minds, why there was one Jew less in the world.

Such is the story as it appeared in the outset. By and by there began to be others. There was a story that this Jesus who had been "hanged on a tree" had risen again from the dead; and this story began to make converts. It was looked upon by the world just as the accounts of modern spiritualism are now, but it spread unaccountably. Three thousand in one day were infected by it. Then the chief priests and authorities tried persecution. It only spread the faster. The converts were in an ecstasy of joy—they rejoiced in tribulation. They gave thanks that they were counted worthy to suffer shame for his sake; and, being driven out of house and home, they went everywhere preaching the word. A young Jewish lawyer, the foremost among the persecutors, suddenly became an enthusiastic believer, gave up his home, his friends, his patrons, his positions, all his prospects of making money or gaining honor, simply that he might preach this story. He said, "What things were gain to me those I counted loss for Christ; yea, doubtless and I count all things but loss for the excellency of the knowledge of Christ Jesus my Lord, for whom I have suffered the loss of all things and do count them but dung that I may win Christ."[4]

From henceforth Paul was a missionary! What Board supported him? What salary was guaranteed to him? None—he wanted none. In accordance with the sensible rule of Jewish education he had been taught a trade. He was a tent maker, and doubtless a very good one. He had learned the trade, probably, in simple conformity to Jewish rule, without any expectation of using it in his own support, as his worldly prospects were fair for a distinguished and honorable position. When he threw that all away for Christ's sake, he started as a self-supporting missionary. He went from place to place, joining

Episcopal Church in Mandarin, Florida. State Library and Archive of Florida.

those of his own craft, making himself useful enough to pay his board, and preaching Christ as he worked, and on Sabbath days in the synagogues, in evenings after work hours, and so gathering in one place and another little churches which he cherished and cared for—as he says, "We were gentle among you, even as a nurse cherisheth her children." In this way he founded churches all through Asia Minor, churches which were dear to him as life blood, churches for whom he prayed daily, and for every member of which he had a sensitive affection. He says, "Who is weak and I am not weak? Who is offended and I burn not?"[5]

Now, is the day of such missionaries past? Is there no call for it? Let us look, for example, at this State of Florida. Here are tracts of hundreds and hundreds of miles which are covered with a sparse and scattered population of people living without churches, schools, or means of culture or improvement of any kind. Take one district, for example. The east bank of the St. Johns River, from Jacksonville up to Enterprise, a distance of 100 miles in length and 18 in breadth, is a district very nearly without Gospel or means of grace of any kind. The Methodists and the Episcopalians, since the war, have sent missionaries through this country who preach, perhaps, once a month at a settlement. For the rest of the time, the people are left to themselves. To give a more particular view of what the state of things is, we will select the little village of Mandarin, from which we write. The village proper consists of a dozen houses scattered along a high bluff on the banks of the river, and perhaps as many more families settled within a distance of six or eight miles. Here a church and school building has been erected by the Freedman's Bureau within the past year.[6] A school is taught for whites six months, and for blacks six months, in the building, the master being supported by the State money. Sunday services have been kept up for nearly two years in Mandarin, during the winter months, and this is the only approach to anything like stated ministration of the Gospel for a circuit of fifteen miles around.

Since the war, this land has been rapidly taken up by young enterprising men from the Northern States, who are clearing it up for the planting of orange and lemon groves, and of peach and almond orchards, and of vineyards. They are men of small capital, who have a hard work to do in clearing up the forests and bringing their farms into a productive state, and this work absorbs all their strength and all their means, and leaves them little to pay for any public enterprise, and it is in vain to expect them to support a minister who yet can hardly support themselves. The native Floridians are many of them Roman Catholics or utterly indifferent to religion and to education.

Yet the people in all this region are gentle, mild, hospitable, always courteous to welcome strangers, ready to listen to religious teaching, always treating it with respect and attention. The blacks have gatherings and religious meetings frequently among themselves, but as their preachers are ignorant, some of them not even knowing how to read, their meetings do not advance them much. Ignorant, ill-informed religious sensibility is apt to degenerate into superstition. There is, within seven miles of Mandarin, a settlement of about fifty black families on government land.[7] These people are very desirous of having religious instruction. They want a school among them. When they laid off their allotments of land they reserved a place for a church, where they built a temporary booth and where they have prayer meetings and occasional preachings.

Now this district is a fair picture of what Florida is morally. Let us suppose a missionary like Paul to come to the ground—a man self-sustaining, who brings the Gospel free, who enters house after house telling of Jesus, who makes himself the tender friend of each family, bearing their burdens, caring for their cares, preaching as he finds opportunity, but mostly carrying the message from house to house and from individual to individual.

A few facts may be given of the experience of one minister of the Gospel who has, so far as his health would permit, tried to do this work.

Professor C. E. Stowe has for six months past maintained stated preaching in the church at Mandarin, and visited, on foot, all the families for a circuit of about seven miles around, entering into every house and forming the acquaintance of the inhabitants. In every case he has been most kindly and hospitably received, found a simple people, gratified with his visit, and ready and pleased to enter into conversations.[8]

In the course of these visits, some touching little incidents have occurred. Walking one day in a wild, secluded place, along the St. Johns River, he came across what seemed an infant's grave, fenced in rudely, covered with little garlands and crosses of flowers. On inquiry, he found the next house inhabited by a family from Maine, whose young married daughter had buried there a beautiful little boy. Mr. Stowe had remarked this family as constant attendants at his Sunday services for some time back. The grandfather took him aside, and, seeming much affected, said to him, "Sir, my daughter's dear little boy died last fall, and there was no minister of any denomination anywhere round, and we had to lay him in the ground without any funeral. Won't you come down some time and have a service for him?"

The family, as it appeared, were Free-will Baptists, and this yearning after the consoling ordinances of religion was the more remarkable in a sect as remote as possible from ritualism.[9]

At their request, notice was given after church, and a little band of friends and neighbors assembled at the house; hymns were sung and consoling passages of Scripture read and the family commended to God.

This one incident shows what the work of a missionary might be, and how many openings the trials and loneliness of new settlements present to the consoling ministrations of the Gospel.

This spring, the Episcopal missionary of the St. John's [diocese?] sent word that he could come and hold a service with us on Good Friday evening. It was deemed, at first, very doubtful whether a congregation could be gathered together. Professor Stowe, however, announced it in all the houses in the vicinity, and was surprised to see that the idea of an evening religious meeting seemed to awaken interest. One old negro patriarch, a most respectable man, who is managing a thriving little farm three miles from Mandarin, said, Oh yes, they would be glad to come—that they always kept Good Friday as a day of fasting and prayer. On asking who taught them, he said it was a Baptist missionary that came over from England years back.

The meeting in the evening was fully attended. The missionary spoke on the seven last words of Jesus on the cross—seven short addresses with a few verses of hymn—singing between them—and it was a most solemn and tender service.

On Easter Sunday the little church was adorned with white Florida lilies, which here grow in the low lands, and with large bunches of shining magnolia leaves, with the white bells of a beautiful flowering huckleberry; and the communion was administered in the Episcopal form by a clergyman from New York, to a small band of different denominations. The majority were Episcopalians, but Baptists and Methodists and Congregationalists were there also, some black and some white, who knelt together at the altar. One of the communicants said it was nine years since such an opportunity had been presented to her. The administration, even to a small circle, seemed like setting up Christ's banner in a place where it had not been planted before. The sacramental service was all the property of one person, who brought it to Florida in hopes that there would be an opportunity to consecrate it to its proper use. It had been resting more than a year, while friends had been struggling to get up a building and to get preaching established, and this Sunday was the first opportunity of using it.

Now, are there not in New England educated ministers, with a competence for their own support, who, if they should come and settle in Florida, might carry the Gospel, without charge, through a whole neighborhood, until society is so organized that there could be then a self-supporting church? In New England, preaching is a luxury, and a man who retires from it feels that there are enough to do work without him, and he can scarcely get a pulpit to preach in if he wants to preach. People in New England are over-preached to. They are like overfed children. The Gospel must be got up as cake and ice cream, to tempt a palled appetite. Here the Gospel is as bread to the perishing.

Multitudes are daily flocking to Florida to make money. They will abandon all the conveniences of civilized life and plunge into the wilderness and brave the danger of acclimating fever, the loneliness of a new settlement, all that they may raise oranges, sugar cane and grapes, and make money. MONEY is a reality, it seems. Is CHRIST a reality? Is Heaven a reality? And is there anybody that will come and invest in Florida for the sake of winning souls to Christ? Every interest of this State is going ahead—except its religious interests. The Sabbath is trodden under foot. The steamboats are rushing up and down the river on that day, perhaps carrying loads of Christian professors. Every grocery is a rum shop, and yet this people are worth saving. Is there any one who will come here as Paul went to the Thessalonians, and say to the people: "So being affectionately desirous of you, we were willing to have imparted to you not the Gospel of God only, but also our own souls, because ye were dear unto us. For ye remember, brethren, our labor and travail, for, laboring night and day, because we would not be chargeable to any of you, we preached unto you the Gospel of God."[10]

And again, in the second epistle to the Thessalonians, he says: "Neither did we eat any man's bread for naught, but wrought with labor and travail night and day that we might not be chargeable unto any of you. Not because we have not power, but to make ourselves an example unto you to follow us."[11]

Would not such preaching of the Gospel as this do more to put down skepticism than armies of books?

People talk of modern skepticism! What was the skepticism that Paul encountered, and how did he overcome [it]? Who thought of believing in Jesus, when he [Paul] came to the great, rich, gorgeous city of Rome, and what was he, one poor man, with his old, worn cloak and his bare hands, against the great, wise, cultivated Roman empire? But he said, I am not ashamed of the Gospel of Christ—it is the power of God and the wisdom of God to every one that believeth. Paul met unbelief with belief—and Christ's church must face modern unbelief with BELIEF. Either what we profess is true or it is not true. If it is true, let us act as if it were.

Notes

1. Based upon democracy: Charles Beecher said as much, "If we look at the question of emigration in a moral aspect, we find much to interest us. Every sober, industrious, religious emigrant is a precious addition to the state [of

Florida], and an element of the best kind of reconstruction. Nowhere can a Christian do more good by a consistent walk and conversation than in Florida, where society is in a forming stage and where schools, churches, and other important institutions are in so large measure to be founded." *Old and New*, Vol. 1 (178-181).

2. Maples: see his book *Dead Men Do Tell Tales.*
3. The article was originally published as "Amateur Missionaries for Florida," *Christian Union*, May 21, 1870.
4. "What things were gain to me those I counted loss for Christ": Philippians 3:7.
5. "We were gentle among you, even as a nurse cherisheth her children.": 1 Thessalonians 2:7; "Who is weak and I am not weak?": 2 Corinthians 11:29.
6. Freedmen's Bureau: a federal agency established in the wake of the Civil War to aid refugees and African Americans. It provided many resources for the construction of schools to communities.
7. Government land: homesteading was common in nineteenth century Florida just as it was in many western states.
8. C. E. Stowe: Mrs. Stowe's husband, Calvin Ellis.
9. Free-will Baptists: a group that combined a belief in salvation for all and a rejection of John Calvin's notion of predestination.
10. "So being affectionately desirous of you, we were willing to have imparted to you.": 1 Thessalonians 2:8.
11. "Neither did we eat any man's bread for naught": 2 Thessalonians 3:8.

A Response to an Obnoxious Reporter

Harriet Beecher Stowe's status as a celebrity earned her a dubious honor at the beginning of her involvement in Florida—the New York Tribune *sent veteran reporter Solon Robinson to describe her activities in Mandarin.*[1] *The journalist brazenly justified his behavior. Stowe "has become, according to our ideals, public property, having written a book, which the public has bought and paid for, and, of course, now has the right to know everything connected with her private life." Robinson outrageously added that the public should "know whether she is squandering the money acquired by authorship." With this mindset, the reporter surveyed the Stowes' property with the care of a bank loan officer. "At the foot of the [live oak] trees, we find a one-story, rough-board building about 16 x 24, divided into two rooms, one having a fire place. Upon each side of this building there is a shed roofed 'lean to' large enough for a bed-room, dispensing with unnecessary furniture." After adding information, he turned to the dining room with a small kitchen, a short distance from the main building. Robinson then claimed that the kitchen had space for the cook to "stand up" if she kept "utensils out of doors." Nothing seems to have escaped Robinson's prying eyes—the barn and outbuildings, the size and number of orange trees, and the profit the citrus crop could generate. Having experience as an agricultural reporter, his estimates were realistic and very positive. He assigned little cash value to buildings and strong ratings for the orange grove. Robinson concluded that Stowe could easily sell the property in Mandarin for profit.*

The insensitive reporter annoyed the novelist. A year later, when the same newspaper published a baseless rumor, Stowe seized the opportunity. She attacked both the unsubstantiated claim and the petty behavior of the reporter. If the novelist lived now, she would sympathize with the plight of the famous—people abused by the press and paparazzi.[2]

Editors of papers and other public characters enjoy peculiar advantages. Self-knowledge is considered a desirable thing, and persons of this sort are in the way of getting it if the public can give it to them. They are constantly enlightened as to their whereabout and what-about in every public journal.

One paper [the *New York Tribune*] that we took up a year or two ago announced that we were making our everlasting fortune by an orange-grove, and gave some startling particulars we had never heard of before. Forthwith it became necessary for the public to be enlightened, and a press-reporter came down at once to our humble cot [cottage], was hospitably received, spent one or two days in investigation, and, going away, after the manner of his tribe, printed all the particulars of his visit, and all the information with regard to our own private and personal affairs, with which an unguarded and hospitable reception made him tolerably familiar. He described our cottage as it then was with a faithfulness to detail that was amazing. Not a knot-hole, not a crack, not a loose board escaped him; he even particularized where we kept our ash-pan, that our dearest friends might lack no interesting item. Never had we received so clear a knowledge of our own property before! We cut out the article and kept it in our pocket, and whenever we were at fault about the length and breadth of a room, the height and thickness of a board, the width of a crack, there we had it. We, in fact, should have not known what it was that the cracks behind the wall-paper were caulked with had not Mr. Solon [Robinson], with praiseworthy industry, extracted the fact from our well-beloved cousin, who had taken upon herself the task of making the little cabin habitable.[3]

Yankee housewives have such a knack of making every thing look well, and they had so befurbished, and bepapered, and becurtained what they found as a little board shanty, that we should have been in danger of looking on it as a regularly plastered room had not Mr. Solon [Robinson] ascertained these precise statistics.

Also, he informed all the world of the exact sums expended in purchase, and with amiable generosity, going back to the year before, related the precise sum lost by an unfortunate investment in cotton-planting. Our agent had not written a particular on that subject even to his parents and nearest Northern relatives; but owing to Mr. Solon's untiring industry and admirable openness, their curiosity was first satisfied by reading these private details in the *Tribune*. Thus we see that, owing to the institutions of news-paper reporters, self-knowledge has wide roots.

A man may think he knows how he looks, and how his house looks, and how his affairs stand, and how he manages, but the best of us are liable to illusions.

It needs a calm, dispassionate observer to come into your house, note-book in hand, observe, weigh, measure, ask questions, put this and that together, and finally print an impartial, minute, dispassionate statement in the *Tribune*. Then, and not till then, do you understand your position!

Should Mr. Solon come down again, he would see that his sketch still needs altering. The little cot [cottage] is like a daguerreotype-sitter that has moved his place.[4] The public are in danger of sinking into apathy at having many ideas. Who will tell them that the little "lean-to" so faithfully described by Mr. Solon has been torn away, and replaced by a two-story erection, of ample dimensions, wedded to the old house? Who will make the public aware that the "loose boards overhead" have been replaced by lath and plaster, and, in fact, that the industriously described little shanty is now a thing of the past? If Mr. Solon were here now, he could tell that the house is yet but half finished; that there is a joiner's bench in the yard with profuse shavings; that there are no locks on our doors owing to the native innocency of our Florida neighbors, and that, consequently, every high wind blows them open in the night, when we amiably get up and pile trunks against them. But, even should Mr. Solon minutely tell all this, still our darling public might not exactly understand the truth; for even while we speak [write] our carpenter-in-chief announces that he is going to give up a day to puttering—which means putting on locks, catches, and all those things of the astonishing number of

The Stowe Residence in Mandarin, Florida: photograph. State Library and Archive of Florida.

which nobody is aware till he builds a house. So hard is truth to be come at; and in view of this, one trembles to think how little history must be worth. When even industry like Mr. Solon's only gives the partial and the temporary, what hope about history which has been written by a whole batch of Solons?

The last effort to enlighten the public comes in the startling news that we have sold our plantation and abandoned the whole thing. What we have sold it for we have not been informed. Can any one tell us? Why we should sell, also has not been made clear to us. Perhaps because last winter was a cold one, and half the orange crop was frozen! But do people up North sell their railroad stock every time a car is smashed up? On examining the Northern papers, we find record of two of these little proceedings, which, probably, in the past two weeks, have sunk more money than all that was lost in oranges in the whole State of Florida last winter. Will they all forthwith sell railroad stock for a mere song, and pour down here to Florida to invest in oranges? One thing is about as reasonable as the other.

But man is a creature of habit. He doesn't so much mind losing money if he only loses it in good, old-established ways. It is an established custom to lose thirty or forty thousand dollars once every two or three years on a railroad; so they make nothing of it. But in Florida, you understand, every thing must pay: pay at once; pay directly; pay certainly, or investment is folly.

If it can be proved even possible not to make money in Florida, or if any thing can be lost, why, pull up stakes at once and go.

We will inform our anxious readers that so far from being dismayed with the last winter's cold, the Floridian agriculturists were never in better heart. It was a gentle tap of Nature on their knuckles saying over her spectacles the time-worn proverb: "My son, don't put all your eggs in one basket." Like sensible men, they took the hint, and are setting out vineyards and peach-orchards; so that if one thing fails, another may not. Moreover, they are deeply enriching their land, and they are planting melons, cucumbers, tomatoes, rice, sweet potatoes, and sugar-cane; so that if one thing won't do, another will. The melons of Florida alone might make it famous, let alone every other consideration. Till people have eaten one of our melons they are in darkness. They have heard of melons by the ear, but they know nothing about them. It is our great, our sublime mission to teach the world what a melon is!

Now, finally, as to this question of losing orange-trees by cold, what are the chances? Why, in 1835, the orange-trees all through Florida were killed to the ground.[5] The grove under which we are writing, for one; yet this grove has been in full bearing order now for twenty years. The roots threw up new shoots, and the shoots are the trees of our present grove. We have just been down with our tape-line and measured six trees whose trunks are over a yard in circumference, which have grown since 1835 from the old roots. For twenty years have these trees been bearing generous crops—they were over with the little accident, and well at it in five years after it occurred. And are we all going to drop our roots and run from Florida because there was a frost last winter or a frost in 1835?

The frost in 1835 was as much an interruption of the ordinary course of things as the earthquakes in California, yet nobody tumbles their Panama stock into market because the whole isthmus may be sunk by an earthquake.[6]

It may, to be sure, as well as the city of Lisbon; and if it is, so much the worse for the stock. Nothing in this world is a certain investment except the Kingdom of Heaven.

There we cannot lose what we put in, and earthly losses may even help our account.

People also talk as if nobody in Florida must be allowed to be sick of any thing or to die, if it is to be considered safe to emigrate there.

People in Northern States may have any variety of fevers. They have typhoid in every country town in Massachusetts and Connecticut at certain seasons of the year. Fever and ague is in New York and New Jersey and on the Schuylkill, but nobody thinks any thing of it.[7] But the very idea that a man may have a fever in Florida is not to be borne. "So much for your old country! A man died in it, to my certain knowledge, and two or three had severe attacks of bilious fever. [8] Your carpenter was sick, was he? So much for your old State."

But we never professed that this was the actual

Land of pure delight,
Where saints immortal reign.

People will have bilious fevers here if they don't take good care of themselves, and being sick, may die here as well as in New-England. Typhoid fevers, however, are almost unknown, and the bilious fever is manageable, and not in general dangerous.

No, we are not going to sell our place and leave our dear orange-trees; and should they freeze to the ground again, though we should weep over them, we should expect to see them doing pretty well in five years and in good bearing in ten, and meanwhile we would live on peaches, melons, and sweet potatoes, sugarcane, and rice.

We have peaches of the size of a butternut [squash] on a tree at our back door. A peach-orchard set out last fall has made shoots two feet in length. Our grape-vines set out in January have canes from two to three feet long, and in a year or two you shall hear from them.

Notes

1. Robinson wrote two articles. The first on March 5, 1868, described the Stowe property and the second on March 14 highlighted Florida's agricultural potential.
2. Originally published as "Under the Orange Trees" in the April 24, 1869, issue of *Hearth and Home*.
3. Cracks were caulked with moss. *New York Tribune*, March 5, 1868. The cousins associated with the Mandarin property were the brothers and sisters of Harriet Ward Foote Hawley, Mrs. Stowe's first cousins through her mother.
4. Daguerreotype: an early form of photograph.
5. In the freeze of 1835, a low of seven degrees was recorded in St. Augustine in February.
6. Panama stock: early investments in the French company that tried and failed to build the Panama Canal.
7. Ague fever: a medical term that referred to bouts of fever, sweating, and chills. It seems probable that this would have included malaria.
8. Bilious fever: an archaic medical term referring to nausea, vomiting, and fever.

Letter from a Verandah

The following article is extraordinary for two very different reasons.[1] Written less than two years after Stowe's railroad trip to Florida, it documents the efforts of steamship companies to improve their vessels. A decade later, in 1886, the Clyde Line would begin service between New York, Charleston, and Jacksonville.[2] The elegance of its shipboard staterooms, dining rooms, and lounges were unrivaled by Pullman railcars. Into the 1930s, many wealthy tourists chose sea passage over other forms of travel. Stowe begins with a very different topic—she joyfully describes the natural world that surrounded her own porch. To just be in Florida brought its own special magic.

Once more it is done. We have stepped from cold winds and leafless trees back into the summer land. Arriving on the eighteenth of November we found the same summer, apparently, that we left when departing on the first of June. The rooms [in our house in Mandarin] were open and airy, and, thanks to "Aunt Katy," clean and in order, three or four vases of roses, chrysanthemums and lilies brightened up the brackets, and the thermometer in the shade of the lime walks, and the verandah stood at eighty-two.[3] The same soft, fresh sun and river breezes were breathing back and forth between the broad St.

Johns and the ocean, and we settle down at once into the verandah life.

Yet it is autumn here. The deciduous trees have lost their leaves; the feathery cypresses, so brilliant in metallic spring green when we left, now have turned brown and sere [burnt] and stand ready to cast off their last year's array. All along the low lands fronting our row of Mandarin houses are the gigantic skeletons of weeds that have run their course—great, succulent, summer monsters whose growth begotten of August fires and swamp mud has been rapid as that of Jonah's gourd; pig-weeds that would frighten Northern pig-weed out of countenance, with a trunk like a strong man's arm and an array of branches where the fowls of heaven might rest.[4] There, too, the skeleton remains of armies of coffee beans—a weed with a most respectable name, of a fine, handsome foliage and an amazing proclivity for growth, yet cursed through all the moods and tenses by Southern cultivators because it bears neither coffee nor any other edible or drinkable fruit, but simply grows and flourishes on its own account without care for the larder of man.[5]

By the way, how astonishing is the arrogance of man, in his contempt for everything that cannot be pressed into his own bodily service. If he can neither eat a thing, drink it nor wear it, nor make it in any capacity his minister, then what right has it to be? Away with it from the earth! The swamp front of our house is full now of dead generations of growths that have had their day under the heats of this summer and passed away. Great, brilliant, tropical flowers, surnamed "blazing stars," have blazed away here with none to see them; convolvuli have twisted and twined and blossomed and seeded, run their course and died.[6] Lush swamp grasses, cat-tails, and fox-tails, and grass banners of unknown name are standing sere and dry.[7] Whole billows of large purple asters still keep up their blossoming, and here and there in the swamp may be found, if one will venture in for it, a starry cluster of St. John's lilies.[8] But, on the whole, the aspect of the low land is ragged and untidy. We miss the sharp-edged frosts of the North which cut and shrivel and clear away the rubbish of the past. We need a definite dividing line in the seasons and to know just when one ends and the other begins.

The oranges have not yet attained their full golden hue—some are yet of a pale green, others of that tawny hue which seems like a sunburn, but the greater proportion this year promise to be bright. They hang in great clusters, six, eight or ten in a bunch together, weighing down the branches like lumps of gold. The wood of the orange tree is the toughest and most resistant in the world—made on purpose to bear these weights of oranges through high winds and tropical tempests. Seldom have we known a branch to give way, however heavy the weight and however strong the wind.

The gray moss on the great live oaks has kept on growing, and the branches now waving before our windows are all a silvery network hanging in graceful festoons.[9]

The living moss as it grows from the tree has a beauty and grace that the dead moss only reminds one of, but cannot equal. It seems full of life to its lightest tips and the delicate, pearly, greenish white of its hue is entirely different from the dull gray of the dead. But moss is a most untidy factor in the Southern life. It would take a man with nothing else to do to pick up the incessant litter a great live oak makes. These great old heavenly monsters from their cloud-world up there are constantly casting down sticks and twigs and branches and bunches of moss, bestrewing the earth with unsightly fragments.[10] Once a year it sends off all its thousands and thousands of leaves, and at another time, its innumerable myriad of acorns rattling down in an unceasing daily and nightly rain. If you don't like it, what are you going to do about it? What are you in the presence of this great king of heaven?—this mighty monarch whose root is in the earth but whose dwelling place is in the clouds—whose branches are a great firmament—whose communings are with skies and stars and all celestial things. Talk to him about littering your door-yard; what right have you to be there at all? Your house, as you call it, looks like a rabbit hutch and you no bigger than the rabbit. He was here rejoicing in the habitable parts of the earth long before you were born—he will be here long after your dust has gone back to the earth as it was.

For our part, we are glad that there are trees so mighty that they humble the pride of man and laugh at the axe of the woodman. To cut down a tree twenty-five feet in circumference, of oak hard as wrought iron, is something that makes even the stupid and ignorant human being pause. If he cannot reverence that which he did not create and cannot restore—that which so speaks of the dignity, power and glory of God who made him, at least he can appreciate the labor and danger and uselessness of the attempt to destroy it. So our three great live oaks, we trust, will live to tell their story to generations after us—when the cottage at their roots has moldered back to dust.

We have here to meet us the usual number of letters inquiring about Florida—three from ladies of infirm health desiring a winter in Florida as a recuperative agency.[11] They want to know, again, is there any opening by which a woman could support herself. We can only answer from our own neighborhood. We believe a competent dressmaker might find employment and support here. In general, any woman who has any well-defined womanly talent can make a support in Florida if she be independent of popular prejudice and willing to work in any line.

A good cook would undoubtedly find warm welcome and good wages among the numerous hotels and boarding houses. There is great demand for skilled, intelligent labor in all the departments of household life.

Moreover, there are many invalids coming South, often obliged to come alone, and it seems to us that positions could thus be found for others desirous of coming. Many who wish to come are in tolerable health and would continue so in this balmy climate, and these could be companions and ministers to those more enfeebled.

By advertising in some public papers, such as the *Christian Union*, or the *Congregationalist*, or the *Advance*, persons desiring attendance and aid might gain the companionship and assistance of those willing to give it.[12]

In regard to the facilities for getting here, we must say, all things considered, we are increasingly convinced that the best and easiest way is that by water.

This year we came on the Charleston boat, and, though we had unremitting head winds, yet our boat, the *Champion*, was so staunch and steady and so well managed that we felt perfect security. At Charleston we merely walked a few steps to find ourselves safe on the *City Point*, which stops at our own door. The next morning after leaving Charleston found us at the wharf in Savannah where we lay till near noon.

We walked up into the town and through the charming succession of little parks on Bull Street to the large park at the end. The grand central avenue which runs through the Park has been prolonged [extended] into an additional tract of ground beyond it, where has been erected a beautiful monument to the Confederate soldiers who fell in the late war. In general style of architecture it resembles the monument to Walter Scott in Edinburgh. The details of it are man-

The Steamship *Dictator* in Charleston harbor. State Library and Archive of Florida.

aged with a justness of taste and moral feeling—a pathos, which must appeal to every heart. What strikes us most is the solemn brevity—the absence of verbiage—the noble calmness which characterizes the whole.

On the pinnacle of the monument stands the angel of the resurrection with the trumpet that is to awaken the dead.[13] Below stands Death, represented by a veiled figure with drooping head and the finger of the right hand laid on its lips, while the other holds the reversed torch—thus suggesting the calmness, the silence, the repose of the grave. The inscriptions are simple and brief.

On one side:

> "Our Confederate Dead":

On the other, the words, from Ezekiel xxxvii., 9:

> "Come from the four winds, O breath, and breathe
> upon these slain that they may live."

Read in the chapter from whence they are taken, these words have a most impressive and pathetic significance. They speak of a nation one in blood, one by every holy tie that should unite men, who had been embittered and contending; they speak of a day when these contentions shall cease in an eternal unity:

"And I will make them one nation in the land upon the mountains of Israel, and they shall no more be two nations neither shall they be divided into two kingdoms any more at all."[14]

All forces of life and nature and society tend to healing. Flowers grow over battlefields, kindness and good will spring up where alienation has been, and the veiled figure with the finger on the lip is the fittest emblem for a monument that perpetuates the memory of a strife among brothers.

Now as to the traveling facilities this fall.

The *City Point* and *Dictator* have both been entirely overhauled and rearranged this summer and are in fine order.[15] We can say this from personal observation in regard to the *City Point*, which we found all bright, clean and shining with new paint, new carpets and new furnishings of all sorts. It was a comfort to know that $18,000 which had been spent in rearranging this boat had not all gone for ornament, but that there had been a complete reinforcement in those lower regions where it is so important to us that a boat should be strong. Passengers who take either the *City Point* or *Dictator* may be sure that they are strong boats, under the most skilled and faithful officers, and no pains are spared on the part of every official down to the very lowest to give the traveler a pleasant and cheerful introduction to Southern waters.

The boats, in order to pass the bars at Fernandina and the mouth of the St. Johns, must of necessity be of lighter draft than the steamers from New York to Charleston and Savannah. For this reason the motion in a heavy sea is apt to be unpleasant. For any one who dreads this motion, the *Lizzie Baker* which takes the inside passage through the Sea Islands is especially to be recommended.[16] It is a pleasant, well-managed boat, and sets a good table; and the opportunity which it gives to see a very curious phase of Southern scenery should not be overlooked by one wanting to learn as much as possible in as little time. All things considered, we regard these three boats as affording the safest and most agreeable entrance into Florida.

We never cross the St. Johns bar and enter the wide blue waters of the St. Johns without a thrill of admiration and almost triumph—it is a sensation which it would be a pity to lose. There is the bar, with its white caps, its roaring breakers, through which the boat moves on the one invisible line which is the only safe channel. She quivers and trembles and sways and tosses, but keeps on and on, guided by the pilot's eye, till in a joyous moment the breakers are past, the tossing ceases, and the boat moves tranquilly into the calm blue sea of the St. Johns. It reminds one of that other passage, seemingly so dreadful, through which we must all pass some day, to the land of eternal flowers and the fountain of eternal youth.

Notes

1. Published with this title on Dec. 8, 1875, in the *Christian Union.*
2. Davis, *History of Jacksonville*, 367; undated images of the interiors of Clyde Line steamships can be seen on line.
3. "Aunt Katy": a generic reference to an African American servant.

4. Jonah's gourd: a fast-growing vine that covered Jonah's shelter in a night; pig-weed: a relative of spinach and chard.
5. Coffee beans: an erect annual, growing over six feet in height with shiny, brown beans.
6. Blazing stars: also known as fairy wands for their "long flower clusters that taper to a graceful, drooping tip"; convolvuli: a vine that resembles a morning glory.
7. Cat-tails: an aquatic weed with long, linear, thick leaves; fox-tails: one of at least six varieties. They have seed heads with short bristles somewhat like a bottle brush; grass banners: long grass blades.
8. Purple asters: flowers have many thin petals around a large central disk. The name is based upon the Greek word for star; St. Johns lilies: probably a reference to St. Joseph's Lilies or amaryllis.
9. Festoons: a decorative banner hanging from two places.
10. Bestrewing: littering.
11. Infirm health: tuberculosis was a major health problem in the period. It was the reason that John Sanford Swaim moved to Jacksonville.
12. The *Christian Union* was, of course, published by Stowe's brother, Henry Ward Beecher. The *Congregationalist* and the *Advance* were other religious periodicals of the period.
13. This description does not match the Confederate Monument in Forsyth Park, Savannah, as it currently exists. A bronze statue of a soldier by David Richards was placed on top of the column in 1879.
14. "And I will make them one nation in the land upon the mountains of Israel," Ezekiel, 37: 22.
15. According to the Photographic Archives of the State of Florida, the "*Dictator* was built in Brooklyn, New York, in 1863 by Thomas Stark. It was first registered in New York City with the number of 6622. It is a side-wheeled paddle steamer that had a gross tonnage of 735. It was 205.8' long, 30' wide, with a depth of 8.6.' It burned on the Hillsborough River in December 1884." http:://ibistro.dos.state.fl.us/uhtbin/cgisiris/x/x/0/5.
16. The *Lizzie Baker* was the only steamboat of the Florida and Savannah Line for which Claghorn and Cunningham served as agents. "The *Lizzie Baker* makes weekly trips to Palatka, touching at all intermediate stops." Historical Record of the City of Savannah: Savannah as it is. www.usgennet.org/usa/ga/county/chatham/.

Seasick

After many years of pleasant voyages to Florida, the Stowes' luck ran out in 1876. It happened aboard a new steamship—one driven by a propeller rather than by paddle wheels. The novelist's account is as vivid as it is interesting.[1]

Well, the Southern bird flight of the season is fairly begun. On Saturday, November 18th, our covey shipped on the staunch new steamer *City of Atlanta,* bound for Charleston, S. C.[2] The day had been clear and calm enough in New York, though the knowing ones shook their heads and predicted rough weather outside. This did not prevent a perfect rush and throng of passengers. Every available berth and stateroom was full, and there were forty or so who had no berths and took their chance accordingly.

It is almost pathetic to see the jaunty spirits, the sort of jocular air of enterprise, with which people come on shipboard. Feathers waving, bows and streamers quivering and dancing, fair ladies smiling, little children chattering—all easy and confident, arranging their belongings in the trim staterooms, and holding gay converse with friends, as for a holiday voyage. Here comes a little puss[girl] of some six summers bearing carefully in her arms a Spitz puppy, with his bright round eyes, erect ears, and inconsiderate [inconsiderable?]

pink tongue lolling gaily out of his mouth, all ready for a capital frolic.[3] Baby and puppy seem about equally inexperienced and equally joyous in prospect of the unknown voyage. The saloon, the decks, the staterooms are all crowded and rustling with busy sociability as the friends of the departing are saying their last words.

But now the steam whistle blows, and "All hands ashore" is the word; and those that are to stay at home hurry off and stand waving their handkerchiefs to those that are to go.

The *City of Atlanta* is an elegant new propeller [driven ship], and with her crowded decks she must have been a fine sight as she moved gracefully away from the wharf and addressed herself to her voyage.

For ourselves, having taken this same Southern voyage for nine years without ever a rough or unpleasant passage or a noteworthy experience of seasickness, we had arranged our stateroom, and were all prepared to settle down to the usual history of a somewhat monotonous but quiet three days of alternate sleeping and boating which should land us at Charleston. But as we were going down the harbor the motion of the boat began to strike us as something quite unusual. "Isn't this going to be rather rough?" we inquired. Ten more minutes and the question was answered. We were out in the ocean in the most tremendous gale of the season.

The Professor, who has been an old salt, and considered himself as adequate to any amount of rough weather, succumbed at once and went head first into his berth with an alarming ejaculation.[4] We climbed to the upper berth and fell in with what speed we might, calling to the most invincible sailor of our party to come and hang up our things. The most invincible one came, hung them up speedily, and with mad haste plunged into her own berth, from whence she rose no more that night. The other member of our party, who had gone on deck in all innocence soon found herself in a rolling avalanche of stools and chairs flying from side to side in wild promiscuity. "Why, what is the matter," she cried. "The matter madam," said the first officer, "is that we're in as tough a gale as you may want to see—be thankful you've got a good strong new ship under you," and with that he guided her down to take refuge in her berth. So there were we all prostrated!

But prostrate we would have been thankful to remain. The ship's berths, we take this occasion to say in loud praise, were provided with nice new spring mattresses presenting in this respect a most wonderful contrast to those instruments of torture commonly called berths on shipboard. Nothing would have been an easier couch to rest on if the sea would only have let us rest. But our berths were athwart the ship, and the ship was rolling in what is called the trough of the sea—the most direful of all conceivable troughs. For the enlightenment of any who may feel curious to know the sensation thus produced we can only say that it consisted in standing first on your head and then on your heels for a series of hours, the change being made with a rapidity which gave little time for collecting one's thoughts and that this kind of motion kept up all night.

Nothing was heard but a chorus of groans and wails, the rattling and rolling of chairs and stools which flew from side to side like catapults, with occasional crashes of crockery from the pantry shelves. In the staterooms, valises, shoes, combs, brushes, the water-jugs broken loose went swirling back and forth with dizzy motion.

A call for the stewardess was answered by a stout young fellow who informed us, "Can't no woman keep afoot this night; you must call on me." And if we reflect that there were in the cabin over a hundred passengers, nearly every one of them deadly sick, we must think that these two or three stewards had a hard time of it. The head steward that had sailed with the captain for twenty years was sick; and if an old salt like him was overcome, what shall be said of the despairs and frights and agonies of those staterooms filled with helpless ladies? We heard the moans of one delicate passenger in the opposite stateroom whom the strange motion had thrown into spasms. No woman could get to her to help her, but we saw her borne out between two stewards and lashed upright into a chair placed in the steadiest and most central point of the cabin. A kind young Irish gentleman of the invincible order, the only man among the passengers who was able to keep up, took the invalid in charge and brought her through the night. A veritable St. Christopher he was, putting his youth and health and strength at the service of the poor, feeble, bedraggled, worn-out passengers who were around him.[5]

We have said there were forty passengers without berths. They lay around everywhere that a man could be stretched on the floor of the upper saloon. The lower saloon, too, was covered with mattresses from one end to the other. As the ship lurched the whole of these mattresses, pillows and all, rolled in one tangled mass now to one side of the saloon and then back again in a similar tumble to the other. There was no swearing; not much remark, only from time to time a faint discouraged effort to right the scattered pillows and mattresses. Now and then things occurred which would have been laughable were not everybody too sick to laugh. A peck basket of apples started from a stateroom, tumbling onto its side and spilling out all of the apples, which went bounding and gyrating in the liveliest manner now to this and then to that side of the boat. In vain the painstaking steward gathered them up and essayed to prop the basket with life preservers; the bewitched thing hopped and flew out again, and the apples renewed their wild dances. A valise in our stateroom packed with medicine bottles also sallied forth, going with a bang to the opposite stateroom wall and soon coming back with a bang to hit against our wall, and so back and forth interminably. We heard the crash of glass, but what of it? We reflected that we couldn't help it. As to the hapless little Spitz puppy who had come on board so jauntily in the afternoon, he got tired of living and before morning stretched out his poor little limbs and gave up the ghost.

We heard of it in the morning and thought he had altogether the best of it in his escape. The long wail of the child occurring every now and then in the fearful clatter reminded one of the gay little puss who had come on board so ignorantly happy in the afternoon. Occasionally in the night the first officer spoke an assuring word in at our window. The ship was staunch and all was going right. "If you could only see it, it is splendid," he said, "the waves are breaking above the masthead."[6] We lifted our dizzy head and saw the great white roaring monsters looking threateningly into our stateroom window; that was enough for us.

Sunday morning came grim and cold; all day the gale held on, all day Monday. By Monday, being thoroughly disciplined, and wholly emptied of self, we climbed out of our upper berth and rolled and stumbled out into the upper saloon, where we sat with feet braced and took a view of the scene.

It occurred to us that if ever there were a danger of civil war or other popular excitement the best place to bring people to reason would be to take the leaders of faction on both sides, put them on board a propeller [driven ship] and let them ride out a three-day's gale.

Our word for it, that at the end of that time they would be as meek and lowly and reasonable as heart could desire. None of them would insist on any thing, providing the boat would stop pitching. Of the hundred and forty passengers it could not be told who was Republican and who Democrat. They didn't care who was President or who was going to be. The only hearty sentiment in which they all joined was in declaring that if once off the boat they never, never, so help them Heaven, would be on that [side] or any other again. All spoke of commuting their tickets at Charleston and finishing their journey by train. One energetic individual expressed the determination to go by land if she had to walk all the way on the railroad track.

But Tuesday morning the storm lulled, the sea became as glass, the boat stopped capering and rolling and became as steady as a Presbyterian elder going to church.

Everybody woke up, came out of their holes and dens, were sitting about in comfort and quiet. A chorus of singers struck up on the forward deck and gave all sorts of national airs and melodies. The bonnets, the feathers, and the bows, and the streamers of the first day reappeared, floating gaily in the balmy sunshine. Little Puss came forth with her doll in her arms and with apparently no tears of regret for the hapless puppy!

> He floats upon his watery bier
> Unwept.[7]

In this new and gayer light of earth and sky, and with a halcyon sea beneath us we reconsidered the proposition of going by train. There, in Charleston, was our own well-known, nice, clean, bright, comfortable *City Point* waiting for us with a smooth sea and bright sky, and we had nothing to do but sit quiet on her deck and be landed in peace at our own door.

All our seasick vows dispersed in thin air, and when the Charleston boat touched the Charleston pier we passed our checks [tickets] at once into the hands of obliging and indefatigable Cavado and felt, when we stepped on board the Florida boat, as if we were already at home.[8]

Notes

1. Originally published as "At Sea" on December 20, 1876, in the *Christian Union.*
2. *City of Atlanta*: this trouble-prone ship collided with a barge and sank in 1925.
3. Spitz: a type of stocky dog with a thick coat and a bushy tail.
4. The Professor: Mrs. Stowe's husband, Calvin Ellis Stowe.
5. St. Christopher: the patron saint who administers to needy travelers.
6. Masthead: the top of the mast, suggesting waves of more than thirty feet.
7. "He floats upon his watery bier": a line from John Brainard's "On a Late Loss." The poem can be found in Rufus G. Griswold's *The Poets and Poetry of America.*
8. Cavado: a reference to the Portuguese appearance of the ship's crew.

A Love Story from March

Stowe's belief in a democratic place in the South where all people thrived remains a timeless vision. While she herself never put it into words, her brother Charles came closest: "If we look at the question of emigration in a moral aspect, we find much to interest us. Every sober, industrious, religious emigrant is a precious addition to the state [of Florida], and an element of the best kind of reconstruction. Nowhere can a Christian do more good by a consistent walk and conversation than in Florida, where society is in a forming stage and where schools, churches, and other important institutions are in so large measure to be founded."[1] To bring these "precious people" Stowe wrote Palmetto-Leaves*—but, not content with the book, the novelist kept on writing. By doing this, Harriet Beecher Stowe reveals a love of Florida with an insight rivaled by few.[2]*

Do you ask what news [is] stirring in Florida? Well, the live oaks are casting their leaves, pushed off by the new spring buds, and if you can show anything that makes more of a stir than that, we should like to see it. Three enormous live oaks overshadow our dwelling—the largest twenty feet in girth—with tops high in air like a firmament, from whence depend filmy draperies of gray moss. For a week past a constant rattling shower of leaves has been falling, with every variety of patter and rustle, now swept in eddying gusts by chance winds, and now sailing daintily downward, and falling with a soft little tap upon the roof. It is a bewildering sight to sit and look up into these great hoary, moss-veiled branches, where the mocking-birds, and red-birds, and sparrows are calling and piping and whistling to each other, in every note of the gamut.[3] And then the live oak acorns: How they fall, and fall! lying on the ground, a perfect mosaic pavement of black, glossy little balls, fallen out of the acorn cups. What a provision does nature make for continuance! Thousands of millions of seed germs, every one of which has the capacity of becoming such a wonder and glory as these oaks that now lift up their crown over our house.

We read with a sort of amazed and dreamy wonder of the snow storms of the North. We [in Florida] have been having days that seemed dream-like in their fairness, their stillness. Since the one very cold snap, in December, that cut off our prospective green peas, there has been an almost unbroken continuance of lovely weather. It is weather that entices you to wander up and down in a sort of blissful half-dream. You hear an orange drop, and saunter forth to pick it up. You see a swan-like steamboat crossing the river, and you linger to see her come in. Then you watch the birds as they chitter and flutter and soar. The whole low ground in front of the house is alive with the bustle of wings. The red maple keys quiver and flash as the birds dart in and out.[4] Now a fiery red-bird has got the topmost twig of a young elm, and whistles breezily as he swings, and another red-bird in the top of an elder-tree replies. Soft, misty vapors of green are rising around the bare bushes of the swamp. Of all moments of the year, the loveliest is this, when the coming foliage is like an ethereal cloud of vivid color, and grows brighter and more vivid day by day. We see the young maple leaves leap forth under our eyes. The elm bough on which that fire spark of a red-bird sits is beginning to feather out into leaves. But the cypresses still hang back, though, taking a closer survey by walking down that way, we see the bright green knobs that will burst into green feathers in a day or two. The cypress feathers in early spring are of the most wonderful greenness, the very color which Dante celebrates as the robes of angels, and Fra Angelico paints in his paradise.[5] The house in such days as this is full of light, just the kind of dusky luminousness that used to please us in the houses of Venice. Lovely gleams and effects of color steal in through open doors and windows, and flicker now on a picture and then in trailing vines of yellow Jessamine in the vase of the mantel.[6] It is a verandah day, and the greater part of the time we all sit there, working, reading and chatting.

Every day brings some company—strangers or friends from Jacksonville—who land from the boat, come up to spend a few hours and, go back in the mail boat. All the North appears to be on the move downward. Jacksonville is full, and running over in fact. Wait long enough in Florida, and you may hope to see everybody.

We have been passing a few days at Magnolia on the other side of the river.[7] A large, well-kept boarding house, full of the most agreeable sort of people. While we were there an art exhibition was gotten up, quite impromptu. A lady and gentleman, artists, who happened to be on the spot, contributed a supply of pictures, and the ladies of the establishment turned the exhibition room into a picture by itself. Easels were extemporized of rough boards covered with glistening leaves of holly or magnolia, supporting the pictures, giving at the

Magnolia Springs Hotel in the 1880s. State Library and Archive of Florida.

same time the most effective backgrounds of dark green. Pillars of palmetto leaves rose in each corner. Palmetto stars were arranged over [the] doors and windows, and graceful webs of moss were festooned from point to point. [8] Vases of flowers, of wild plums, and yellow Jessamine, and bright scarlet maple keys stood here and there, while the pictures, tastefully arranged, were so placed that they could be conveniently examined.

There was a tableau of pretty children exhibited in the same room. Besides this we had fine music by different performers, comic songs, readings, etc., making the evening pass off most agreeably.

Magnolia is only about a mile and a half from Green Cove Springs, and we drove over there the next morning to try the celebrated sulphur baths. The spring is a great curiosity. It wells up from a chasm thirty or forty feet deep, between what look like great greenish ribs of sulphur. The temperature of the water is about 78°. It is of a most crystalline clearness and sparkle. It runs into a great bathing tank of about a hundred feet long, surrounded by a high wall overhung by live oak trees. Around, on the inside of the wall, is a girdle of earth walled up from the water, where banana-trees grow, and must cast a beautiful picturesque shade, though the unusual frost of December had now robbed them of their leaves. A row of dressing-rooms on one side are appropriated to bathers, and one descends by steps into the water, which is only about four feet in depth. The day was sunny and calm, and we found the bath most agreeable. The water is so warm as to produce no shock, and buoys one up delightfully.

After the bath, there is a peculiar feeling of refreshment and exhilaration. Very many rheumatics have received great benefit from the constant use of [the baths]: and we found it a common practice for the dwellers at Magnolia to walk or ride over every day to enjoy them. Two large hotels at Green Cove, the Clarendon and the Union, are both full of guests, besides many private boarding houses.

Life at Magnolia and Green Cove seems to consist mainly in living. There is in the delightful, soft, dreamy air of these days something that inclines us to sit in the open air and imbibe; to wander aimlessly; to dream; to feel happy without asking why or wherefore. The young men have yachts, and hunt and fish, but all in a quiet sort of way. The ladies walk backwards and forwards among the cottages that face the river, and sit here and there in groups, chatting, reading, sewing. Children are out from morning till night, gathering violets, ferns, mosses, acorns, and whatever else suits them. Florida is the children's Eden. We envy every child that spends a winter here, for it is so much pure gold of enjoyment put into life. Not the many voices of birds calling to each other from the trees are so sweet as the voices of the troop of gay little ones who play from morning to night about our houses. What a contrast to the confinement, the close-heated rooms, and consequent coughs, and colds, and fevers of northern winters.

January 20 [1873]—Last evening at dusk a party from Jacksonville, in a sail-boat, dropped down upon us just at dusk. They had been all day on the St. Johns trying to get to us; but the delicious hush and calmness of the air proved rather provoking to those who want air-wings to bring them along. After tea, and a chat on the verandah, we lighted a great bonfire from the clearing in front of our house, and had an illumination that made us look like fairy land. The great cavernous dome of the live oaks, with their hanging films and draperies of moss, were lit up with weird red light, and looked like a great grotto with hanging stalactites. The oranges, amid the dusky shadows of the boughs, gleamed out like ruddy gold. By the light of the fire we waited on our friends to the wharf to take sail again. Just so treacherous is this river; sometimes one can come with all ease in two hours [from Jacksonville]; and here a whole day had been spent in vain, and the return must be in the night. We saw them hoist sail; a little breeze sprung up, and away they went.

This morning is like July. The river is lying in a hazy stillness; and, as we sat at breakfast, we saw an alligator swim past the wharf. Mr. T., with experienced eye, first detected the peculiar ripple he made, and the spy-glass verified the fact that it was a big fellow, about twelve feet long, going quietly by. This is sure indication that warm weather is come. No alligator that understands himself would think of taking such an excursion without the most positive assurance of this fact.

For us, we have all been fluttering in muslins and cambrics.[9] Summer garments have a delicious sense of freedom in them! A party of cheerful friends from Magnolia came across in a little steamboat and spent a pleasant hour or two with us, and now they are gone; and the next sensation is the *City Point* stopping at the wharf with all flags flying, and William C. Bryant on board![10] Let the yellow Jessamine and the orange blossoms hear it, and rise up to welcome our poet to the land of flowers.

Notes

1. *Old and New*, vol. 1 (178-181.
2. This article originally appeared as "Sunshine on Southern Shores" in the March 12, 1873, *Christian Union.*
3. Mocking-birds: a southern gray and white songbird; red birds: most likely cardinal.
4. Red maple keys: red maple seeds, papery and decorative.
5. Dante: the medieval Italian poet; Fran Angelico; a Florentine painter of the fifteenth century. Stowe toured Europe in the wake of the publication of *Uncle Tom's Cabin.*
6. Jessamine: a variation of jasmine.
7. Magnolia: the location of a hotel near Green Cove Spring on the west side of the St. Johns river.
8. Palmetto stars: palmetto leaves with numerous star-like points.
9. Cambrics: cambric is a type of glossy cotton.
10. *City Point*: a side wheel steamship built in 1864; William Cullen Bryant: an American Romantic poet and a journalist. In this period he was translating the *Iliad* and the *Odyssey.*

Stowe's Visit to Planter Florida

In 1874, Harriet Beecher Stowe visited Tallahassee, the state's capital and the geographic center of efforts to replicate the Old South. The red clay soil of counties in what was called Middle Florida offered the same potential for raising cotton as had much of Georgia. Decades before the Civil War, affluent settlers brought their slaves from Virginia and Carolinas and created plantations similar to those in neighboring states. It was a very different world than the tourist city of Jacksonville and Stowe's enclave at Mandarin.

The novelist's account of her travel is revealing from both what she said and what she did not say.[1] Planters in Middle Florida had more slaves than farmers in other parts of the state and lost far more capital with emancipation. Local feelings ran deep and thus many citizens prided themselves that Tallahassee, and Tallahassee alone, had been the only state capital east of the Mississippi in the hands of the Confederacy at the end of the Civil War. The novelist traveled as a part of a delegation of businessmen, no doubt reducing the potential of harassment from diehard secessionists.

The stated purpose of the trip—to encourage development and investment—was always a key portion of Stowe's agenda. At this time she also had another. In this article, she never mentions her brother Charles. Yet when her picture was taken on the steps of the state's

Capitol, he is in the foreground. She also mentions wanting to go to Wakulla Springs, and cancels a picnic because of the weather. The distance from the springs and Charles's dwelling at Newport is only a few miles. His service in state government had ended in 1872 and he was living quietly on his farm. By this time he had visited his sister and her family at Mandarin and, without doubt, had invited her to his home. Seeing brother Charles was an important reason for Stowe's excursion into Rebeldom.[2]

The behavior of residents, most of whom were traditional Southerners, is revealing. In spite of their feelings about Uncle Tom's Cabin, *they willingly extended hospitality to her. The prospect of actually seeing the world-famous author outweighed their intense disdain for her book. And while these Southerners rose to the occasion, she misread their goals and intentions. Stowe is hopeful about the future—while many of them were seeking a Jim Crow world that would reinvent the subservience of slavery. Middle Florida would become a center of lynching for decades to come.*[3] *She wrote:*

"You can't judge of Florida till you have seen Tallahassee," a friend has long been saying to us. Tallahassee means West Florida—the region between the Suanee [Suwannee] river and Apalachicola Bay.[4] And certainly there is a difference.

But the fact is that the great broad St. Johns river with its ready made watery high road of travel, has drawn the whole forty thousand who travel to East Florida. It was so easy to get into a steamer at Savannah that would take you in one voyage and without change to Jacksonville, Mandarin, Hibernia, Magnolia, Green Cove Springs and Pilatka [Palatka], that the whole stream of travel has found this way; and the greater part of tourists and residents who have bought winter homes know no other Florida than East Florida. Hence the general concessions that Florida is a flat country with a soil of white sand, and various other impressions, all of which are true of East Florida only.

But the fact is that beside the great ease and convenience of the water travel through the St. Johns, West [Middle] Florida has been shut out of the knowledge of tourists by most uncomfortable and disagreeable railroad arrangements, that seem as if they had been intended expressly to keep people from going there. Hence, while East Florida had been looking up in a wonderful manner, while real-estate in the neighborhood of Jacksonville and Pilatka [Palatka] has risen two or three prices, [Middle] Florida has remained almost stationary. But recently a series of excursions has been projected to take tourists from Jacksonville to Tallahassee, and we have gone with the multitude.

The region about Tallahassee, to the eye of a New Englander, has many points fairer and more home-like and familiar than any Southern country we have yet seen. It is a fine rolling country with high green hills and deep valleys, and beautiful clear lakes, suggesting in some faint degree that part of the Berkshire County in Massachusetts where the undulations of the land first commence.[5] Berkshire County without its winter would certainly be paradise enough for

Governor Marcellus L. Stearns greeting Harriet Beecher Stowe at the Capitol in Tallahassee, 1874. State Library and Archive of Florida.

almost any man or woman, and this is something like it. The soil as a general thing is strong and rich. We give the opinion of an experienced Northern agriculturalist by whose side we rode up and down these hills and valleys. "Clay, well mixed with sand and disintegrated limestone," he soliloquized, "such a soil might grow almost anything."

It is not a region for tropical fruit-growing. The wild orange is not native to this region, and there are few cultivated orange groves. The uncertainty which attends their culture, owing to occasional frosts, renders it unsafe to invest in them other than for purposes of pleasure, as we grow tender fruits at the North. There are large old orange trees of forty years standing in that vicinity, but their number is not great, and they have been much put back and damaged by frosts four or five years ago.

But this fine strong soil is exactly adapted to profitable farming. Corn, cotton, sugar, and all the vegetables that we are familiar with at the North could be raised. What is more to the purpose, our agricultural friend pronounced it to be land that promises a wheat crop as fine and abundant as that of Georgia. Add to this that it is land where growth goes on all winter, and what more could mortal ask? This fine land is now in the market so cheap that the opportunity for investment should not be neglected.

In regard to society, Tallahassee and the region round furnishes many inducements. The large plantations about there were held in many instances by men of good sense and liberal views, who saw the wisdom and propriety of making the best of the situation which the fortunes of war forced upon them. One planter, who had employed six hundred slaves when the emancipation proclamation was issued, called together his hands, and read and explained it to them. "Boys," he said, "this means that you are all as free as I am, and can go when you like, but those that like to engage to work for me for fair wages I will keep"—and the most of them remained.

But these planters are satisfied that the new order of things requires new arrangements. Instead of owning farms of thousands of acres, they are desirous of dividing into smaller farms and adopting more useful modes of culture.[6] Farmers coming among them would receive every encouragement. The land would be furnished to them cheap, or every aid that the older settlers could give in enabling them to adapt themselves to the new conditions of life at the South would be cheerfully furnished.

In fact, the whole object of these excursion parties has been to give to the Tallahassee people an opportunity of expressing their friendly and hospitable sentiments toward strangers from the North.

The arrival of our excursion party at Tallahassee seemed to be a signal for all sorts of hospitable attentions. The flower-gardens of Tallahassee have long been celebrated through the State, and the first morning after our arrival was devoted to the visiting of gardens. In every case they were thrown open to our inspection in the kindest manner, the owners coming out and offering to cut roses and lilies or other floral treasures for us. Tallahassee ought to be called preeminently the city of roses.[7] We have seen fine roses bushes before, but here the rose becomes a tree as large as the lilac-tree in our dooryards, and is covered with an abundance of such splendid roses as are seldom seen. A tree of Marshal [Mareéchal] Niel, Cloth of Gold, La Marque, or Solfaterre is a splendid sight.[8] There was one rose, of which we examined two trees in one yard, which was so singularly beautiful that we should like to know the name of it. It was large and very double; the outside leaves were of a shade of the blackest crimson, the next layer were lighter crimson, the next fine rose-color, which gradually grew lighter and lighter till the center of the rose was a clear white. One agricultural friend told us that the soil of Tallahassee was of the precise mixture and composition adapted to the growing of this queenly flower, and thus its wonderful perfection there is accounted for. Our days in Tallahassee seem a vision of roses. At every garden we entered our hands were filled with buds and roses of the rarest and most perfect kind. We returned to the hotel to find bouquets equally choice had been sent in. Almost every caller and visitor (and there were constant and most agreeable visitors) brought new roses, and in the evening reception given by the citizens to the excursionists there was a bewildering succession of bouquets of the rarest and most perfect flowers. This reception was given as an especial act of hospitality on the part of the city. This large, new, tasteful hall was beautifully adorned with greens and flowers, so as to look like a perfect bower, and "Welcome" in large gilded letters was the inscription that met the eye on entering.[9] There is a very beautiful evergreen called the bamboo vine, of which the green trimmings are made and the wild double multiflora rose from the woods formed long garlands with it. Agreeable, cultivated people and numbers of pretty young girls conspired to give us agreeable impressions of the society. All sorts of kind hospitalities were pressed upon us, and our time to dinner and tea was bespoken for a day or two ahead could we only have remained. In the course of the evening reciprocal speeches of welcome on the one side and of thanks and acknowledgment on the other were exchanged between the citizens of Tallahassee and spokesmen appointed by our party; and when the older people had retired at canonical hours, the younger ones danced till midnight.

The next day a picnic to Wakullah [Wakulla] Spring was to have come off, but an unfortunate storm prevented, and the weather set in so cold that, having started with only thin dresses and hot weather appointments generally, we had to hasten back, leaving unfulfilled hosts of agreeable engagements that would have still further perfected our acquaintance with the hospitable people of Tallahassee.[10]

Before we went, however, we were assembled on the State-house steps of Tallahassee, Northerners and Southerners, and a photographer took a picture of the group as are [*sic*] presentation of the South receiving the North and giving the right hand of fellowship.[11] Let it stand for a memorial. In old times people put up a heap of stones as a witness, and people ate together on it. In our day we all go and are photographed together.

Why should we not be friends? What earthly interest have we now to separate us? The interest of every new settler in Florida must henceforth be that of every old settler; we are helpers of one another. Let there be no strife except who shall raise the finest roses, and there we think for some time to come the people of Tallahassee will bear the palm.

P.S. –Even a Palmetto Leaf is not complete without its P.S. We were happy to hear that a movement has been set on foot for a large and elegant hotel for winter boarders in Tallahassee.[12] It is hoped it will be ready by next winter.

Notes

1. The article was originally published in the *Christian Union* on May 6, 1874, as "A New Palmetto Leaf."
2. Charles Beecher's service as a member of the governor's cabinet is described at length in *Beechers, Stowes, and Yankee Strangers: the Transformation of Florida.*
3. Four lynchings are recorded for Tallahassee, alone, with the last as recent as 1937 when two black teenagers were murdered almost on the lawn of a state supreme court justice. Ernest Powders and Richard Hawkins were removed from jail and shot on August 2, 1937. Their deaths were the topic of an article in the *Florida Historical Quarterly*, vol. 66 (July 1988), 41-59. The judge took no action any more than did the state's disgraceful governor. While Stowe remained hopeful, many traditional Southerners used terrorism to maintain their place atop society.
4. Stowe described all of "Middle Florida" as "West Florida" in the original article. West Florida actually refers to the land between the Apalachicola River and Pensacola.
5. Berkshire County: the county that runs the entire length of Massachusetts along its western border with New York.
6. Many of these plantations were not broken up but sold in the late nineteenth century to wealthy Northerners as hunting preserves.
7. Tallahassee did not market itself as a "rose city" while nearby Thomasville, Georgia, did.
8. The Mareéchal Niel (which Stowe referred to as "Marshal Niel") was, according to T. W. Sanders, "The most popular and universally grown of all climbing varieties [of roses]." *Rose and Their Cultivation*, London: W.W. and L. Collinggridge, 1917.
9. Large, new, tasteful hall: Gallie's Hall.
10. Wakullah [Wakulla] Springs: a Middle Florida rival in size and beauty for Silver Springs.
11. Right hand of fellowship: Stowe's description of the photograph is misleading. The Governor at the time was Marcellus Stearns, who had lost an arm fighting for the Union. A more accurate description would be "Florida's last nineteenth century Republican governor greets Mrs. Stowe."
12. Large and elegant hotel: this is not a reference to the St. James Hotel or to the Leon, two large nineteenth-century hotels in Tallahassee.

Rail Travel to St. Augustine

St. Augustine, with its elaborate Spanish fort, numerous colonial buildings and dwellings, and narrow streets was on the itinerary of many early tourists. To reach the historic city in the 1860s and 1870s by steamboat would have required a circuitous route and negotiating both the hazardous entrance to the St. Johns River and the harbor at St. Augustine. The alternative route in Stowe's time meant taking a steamboat from Jacksonville or as in the novelist's case from Mandarin to Tocoi—a noteless place. Or as she put it, "Tecoi [Tocoi] consists of a shed and a sand-bank, and a little shanty." From here the tourist would catch the St. Johns Railroad to the ancient city. In Palmetto-Leaves *Stowe tells us that she had made the journey three times and offers a very minimal account. The "train" did not have a fixed schedule, so if there were only a few tourists who disembarked at Tocoi you might have to wait for another steamboat or two, something that could take several hours. Once a sufficient number of travelers had assembled, the railroad let them board its only railroad car and then it was pulled by horses. The trip of fifteen miles, according to Stowe, could take up to four hours at the height of the busy tourist season or, as in her experience, it took two. Although the "train" was slightly faster than mosquitoes, the novelist enjoyed taking a careful inventory of the flora.*[1]

We have come over [the St. Johns Railroad] ... each time the varieties of shrubs and flowers, grasses and curious leaves, were a never-failing study and delight. Long reaches of green moist land form perfect flower-gardens, whose variety of bloom changes every month. The woods hang full of beautiful climbing plants. The coral honeysuckle and the red begonia were in season. Through glimpses and openings here and there we could see into forests of wild orange-trees; and palmetto-palms raised their scaly trunks and gigantic green fans. The passengers could not help admiring the flowers; and as there were many stops and pauses, and as the gait of the horses was never rapid, it was quite easy for the gentlemen to gather and bring in specimens of all the beauties; and the flowers formed the main staple of the conversation.[2]

Although Stowe enjoyed traveling on the St. Johns Railroad, many tourists were less enthusiastic. The following article describes a number of improvements in the line and the quirky and unsettling conditions that remained three years later.[3] While a steam locomotive replaced the horses, the number of coaches had increased. Real problems occurred when the line was busy and the company pressed other equipment into service.

The article is also interesting since the owner of the railroad belonged to one of the nation's wealthiest families. It was purchased in the early 1870s by William Astor, who supposedly gave the task of improving it to a son. While the Astors could have obviously foreshadowed Henry Flagler by dramatically improving service, they seem to have gone at a much slower pace. In the late 1880s, they sold the business to Flagler.[4]

People come long distances expressly to see the very worst railroad in the world, and to ride under the excitement of a possible blowup or other catastrophe. It was not a special honor to your correspondent to ride on the water tank with a pine knot for a footstool, for the honor was shared with other passengers, nine in number, two being ladies. The fact is there are but two cars on the road, and they had been monopolized by a firemen's excursion from Jacksonville.

There was nothing left for us but a wheezy old locomotive compounded out of a pumping engine, a dirt excavator and the safety valve of a ferry boat, and a tender which held two 10-gallon water tanks and the product of a wood pile.

I am not proud, and so I mounted. As your representative, I was awarded the seat of honor. The ladies were accommodated with 25-cent chairs from the waiting room; the gentlemen made themselves as happy as they could; the man who could not get on the tender stood up on the platform of the locomotive, where were gathered the baggage and freight. The railway superintendent held on by one hand, the engineer looked out one window, and the fireman out of the other. The whistle was blown six times and then it commenced raining and we all rushed into the depot. Then it stopped and we rushed back again; then the whistle was blown three times more and we started.

Having started, I will tell you something about Tocoi, not much for there is very little to talk about. As you approach it you see two houses and the depot. In one of these is an 'eating saloon' where the guidebooks will inform you, an excellent meal can be had. I will not

The St. Augustine and Tocoi Railroad, 1876. State Library and Archive of Florida.

deny it, in fact I cannot, for the firemen came and carried everything off before I arrived there, so I will take the guidebooks on trust.

It was with a sense of relief that I took my position on the water tank and sat under the master mechanic's blue umbrella. We went for a mile, and I gave vent to a sigh of satisfaction. Then there was a stop, and the engineer called for a hammer. The repairs were expeditiously made, however, and we passed on. Then it was found that the freight was shifting and threatened to capsize the locomotive. We stopped again, and with the assistance of part of the passengers, this was remedied. Then we came to a station where we wooded up; then to another station, where there were three old cars, in one of which hot coffee was held forth as an enticement, but we did not stop. Next two sticks of wood slipped off and I shouted in time to stop the train and save them. The superintendent kindly got off to pick them up, and we went on triumphantly.

The scenery on the line of the road put me strongly in mind of a view of Philadelphia I once saw, consisting of rows of brick houses. Change this to pine trees and you have it. You may add the palmetto with roots like the sea serpent's back.

The inhabitants are not numerous. I saw one alligator with a buzzard hovering over him, wishing he was dead. There was a long stretch of swamp, and out of this the gator thundered in search of a pig. We did not stop to kill him which I wondered at. There may be some residences in the distance but I did not see any.

The mail service is transacted after a novel fashion. When a man wishes to post a letter he splits a stick at the end and inserts the message, then he runs at or after the train and hands it to the conductor.

I spoke of swamp. This is filled up with logs, and the supports for the rails are resting on top. You may believe that going over a swamp a mile or two long, filled with decaying and rotten pine logs is not a cheerful operation. And yet I will tell you a fact, and you must give me credit for downright truthfulness; that I never traveled with a more contented or merrier set of passengers than those on that tender. I believe they positively enjoyed the risk they were running. The engine was slowed to about a mile in five hours; the bridge cracked;

the locomotive groaned; the conductor held on by one hand on one side, the fireman by one hand on the other, while the engineer with a hand on the throttle valve looked out ahead.

And so, as on a sea voyage which comes to an end just as everybody begins to swear eternal friendship to everybody else, so came we to our journey's end, or in sight of it, for the railroad stops a mile short of the town. The nine of us were soon packed into four omnibuses, and we reached our destination.

Elegant structures and orange groves meet us as we go into the city, and less elegant [structures] without the groves are plentiful inside. A great hotel with a monstrous defiance of architecture stands there, all doors and windows like a gigantic pigeon house.[5] The hand of the vandal has been pulling down the coquina houses, which are or were the attraction of the place, and has built shanties, which only proclaim his own bad taste. There are many square walls standing of the old Minorcan building, surmounted by a rough upper story of boards and shingles. I stood in amazement and wondered. I wondered that the state, county and city did not step in and stop the destructive tendency of Americans. St. Augustine should be a perpetual link between the past and the present. While it is too late to restore what has been lost, I should think that self-interest alone would lead to an instant cessation of any further interference with what remains.

Still, though the old city stands a good deal mutilated, there is something to be seen. The old fort is one of the noblest pieces of warlike architecture.[6] While it has no strength to resist modern artillery, it is massive enough to show how powerful a kingdom Spain then was, and how arrogant her assumptions in respect to a country she had not conquered. It is a fort which would have graced any city of the mother country and have bidden defiance to all the world. Moorish in its architecture, it contained all the elements of a city: residences for the soldier, casemates for safety in battle, dungeons for criminals, and a church for God.

St. George Street comes the nearest of any to my idea of what an old Spanish street should be. It is refreshingly narrow, and with some of the old walls left, and the jutting balconies, looks decidedly picturesque. It holds a singular and amusing mixture. A Spanish face projects from one house front, a French from a second, a German from a third, and an American from a fourth. A lady from Maine engineers a boarding house within Minorcan walls, and the sign of a curiosity dealer projects from the doorway of a Spanish cavalier. If you search for one of the ancient sort, the chances are you will tumble upon a French pastry cook, or a German happy over his pipe and his lager. If you find a genuine Spanish face, as I did, you will hear, as I heard, as good English as you ever spoke in your life.

There is one antique gem which I trust will be carefully preserved—a gateway.[7] It is not large or imposing, but is old and quaint, and the few feet of wall on each side are overgrown with grass and bushes. There was evidently a ditch before it, but whether the wall encircled the city I do not know. If it did, it is a great pity it was not preserved. An old market house and the monument in the square, commemorating a liberal Constitution in 1813, are about all that commemorates Spanish possession. Since I came to see the old city, and not the new, I left St. Augustine and went back to Tocoi.

Notes

1. Stowe, *Palmetto-Leaves*, 207.
2. Ibid., 209-10.
3. J. K. Hoyt originally wrote this article as a part of a series. See the Newark, New Jersey, *Sentinel of Freedom*, June 1, 1875.
4. Gregg M. Turner, *A Journey into Florida Railroad History*, 132.
5. Giant pigeon house: the building of grand hotels in St. Augustine was just beginning. Even greater pigeon houses would be built.
6. Warlike architecture: Castillo de San Marcos.
7. Gateway: the city gates near the fort still stand.

Southern Christmas and New Year

In the 1870s and 1880s, Mandarin grew as a center of citrus production in Florida. This article describes the community's transformation from a tiny village.[1] *A local historian reported that "many people, attracted mainly by the prosperous agricultural reports, left their homes in the states and England to settle in or near Mandarin."*[2] *As a result the population grew, reaching over twelve hundred residents. About one quarter were white and the rest were African American. The village would have three stores, three churches, and a public school. All of this growth faded with freezes in the 1880s. Frigid weather in 1894 and 1895 forced the citrus industry to shift over a hundred miles to the south.*

Think of a Christmas sermon with open windows and a rush of waving fans all through the church. Think of putting up Christmas greens on a warm June day! And such greens! Great broad magnolia leaves, shining with richness; holly, with its crimson berries; catbrier vines, light and graceful, and cedar, fine and feathery, with little golden buds on the top of every feather; and then the festoons of airy gray moss.[3] Certainly Christmas dressings are of the best here, where about half of the trees are evergreen. Our little schoolhouse-church is for one day made to look quite festive. Then comes the making of some sixty or more candy bags, to delight our neophyte Christians, old and young, who mingle in the Sabbath school. Christmas eve our school all gather there and make the woods ring. We sing, "Hold the fort, for I am coming," loud enough to startle all the forest echoes; and a right brave, cheery song it is for people that are in a frontier settlement and doing mission work.[4] Then follow Christmas carols proper, and then come the giving of gifts, cake, candy and apples, pictures, books and other trifling gifts—a great deal of delight at very little cost! Everybody seems pleased, and our Christmas eve goes gaily by. But our colored brethren cannot stop at nine or ten o'clock. The singing for them is just begun. All troop out two miles into the woods to their own church and make a night of it. The singing fatigues a white person—it rests a negro. Just at the point where a white person is used up a negro is well warmed up to his work and ready to begin. Singing grows to be an ecstasy, a perfect intoxication; it takes possession of the whole man, and the "*shout*," as it is called, is a sort of a rhythmic dance, in which the tropic blood of the old African origin asserts its difference from our colder race, and displays its more fervid life powers. In olden times, when the day was one unpaid, unremitting toil, and to sing all night restored the weary. The sacred "shout," with its rhythmic melodies and dances, refreshed and rested and brought them round for the next day's toil. Thus birds sing when they are hungry, sing when they are in trouble, and in singing find ease, refreshment and rest. It takes a good deal of philosophic thought to understand the difference of races, and that what suits one race may not suit another. There is no doubt that sacred songs, dances and choruses, which to us are listened to only as a curiosity, have a power to stir the very deepest and best feelings of the colored race to brace them to endurance, courage, patience and hope. The Spirit of God understands all languages, all races, and speaks to every man in the tongue where in he was born.[5]

Our little settlement is a social one. We meet every Saturday and Sunday night to sing, and almost every day besides. Houses stand open; people sit on their verandas, or speak to each other as they pass by. Yet, after all, our settlement is a busy one. All the stronger sex are busy with both hands. A new wharf has been going up in our neighborhood, preparatory to a new house, for which lumber is coming up in daily installments. A barn is building just behind us. The lot back of us is being cleared ready for another house. Everywhere in the pine woods as we ride we see the little new houses of settlers rising, besides trim and respectable houses of colored men, which we are glad to see succeeding to the old log cabins. Our more respectable colored men who have regular wages have at last arrived at the luxury of frame houses, with glass windows, brick chimneys and two stories. A house is an unfailing index of civilization and progress.

Mandarin is about the busiest, the thriftiest, the most industrious community we know anything about. Everybody works, and things appear to be moving on. The tap of hammers wakens us at seven, and keeps on all day a cheery music. The orange orchards that were set out last year have grown finely, not withstanding an unusually hot, dry summer, and for a good mile along the river banks is now one continuous succession of orange groves.

Bless the bountiful orange! It the most generous, the most courageous, the most thrifty, the most large-hearted of trees, and by all means the most beautiful.

If I were to find an emblem of that heavenly charity that St. Paul recommends, it would be an orange tree. It bearth all things, believeth all things, hopeth, endureth all things. It seems almost impossible to kill it. It will grow and flourish and bear golden fruit even in the most slovenly, neglected orchard; but it will grow more gloriously and bear more fruit if it is nurtured; and, like charity, it never faileth.

Our trees are a dream of loveliness now, and we cannot bear to pick the beautiful treasures to ship and send away. We feel miserly. The sight of such lumps and clusters of gold inflames us, and we only resolve of this and that tree that money cannot pay us for it—we must send them to friends as a free-will offering. Our gentlemen, some of them, are shippers. They go about the country and buy the crops on the trees—pick and sell them, paying for them as they stand, and taking all the risk of packing and transportation. This to the distant cultivator is an easy and sure way of disposing of a crop.

Our wharf has been loaded with barrels all the holiday season. Now, however, the tactics of packing seem to be changed, and boxes similar to those in which Sicily oranges are sold are being adopted.[6]

New Year's Day we were invited to the Sunday school picnic festival of the Methodist church in the woods about two miles off. It is a lovely spot by the side of a grove of magnolias. A clear spring boils up from the ground at the roots of the trees; the water, like that of many of our springs, is impregnated with sulphur and iron. In the church a young magnolia tree has been planted upright, and from its branches [descended] oranges, apples, bags of candy, little pictures, and other fine things for the children. A humorous poem was read, giving the obituary notice of the deceased year and welcoming the Centennial. It was from the pen of a Vermont gentleman, one of our recent settlers, was sprightly and amusing, and gave a pleasant opening to the affair. Then Prof. Stowe made a few remarks, saying that it was such a First of January as could hardly be conceived of in the cold North, and expatiated on the advantages of living where the ground could be worked all the year round, where fuel could be had for the picking up, and winter clothing was so light an expense—thence digressing by easy stages into the good, set themes of advice and commendation proper to a Sunday school gathering.[7] Then, for our part, we told the children a story; and after some speech-making, the candy bags and pictures and apples were distributed. Then we all repaired with our baskets to long tables spread under the magnolia trees and arranged our various viands and fell to jovially.[8] The day was perfectly lovely—one of those days that you can think only of heaven as being any more perfect. It was not hot, it was breezy and soft and sunny, and the air was full of birds' voices. It was a day to make it seem pleasant to be alive. There are many days here that are so fair that one only wants to sit still and enjoy—drink in at every pore. It is an unprecedentedly warm winter so far. We have some fears lest it end in a cold snap—but sufficient unto the day is the evil thereof.[9]

The orange blossom buds are beginning to start, and we have planted our first planting of sweet corn. A frost now would be a sad affair—let's hope that it won't come.

To all who want warmth, repose, ease, freedom from care, we cry, "Come! come! come sit on our veranda!"

Notes

1. The article appeared with this title in the *Christian Union*, January 19, 1876.
2. Mary Graff, *Mandarin on the St. Johns*, 73.
3. Catbrier: a climbing plant with a prickly stem and thick leaves.
4. "Hold the fort, for I am coming": a song about the Civil War by Philip B. Bliss.
5. "The Spirit of God understands all languages, all races, and speaks to every man in the tongue where he was born": based upon 1 Corinthians 12:4-12.
6. Sicily oranges: Stowe probably became familiar with these in markets in Europe.
7. Prof. Stowe: Mrs. Stowe's husband; expatiated: explained in detail.
8. Viands: special dishes of food.
9. "But sufficient unto the day is the evil thereof": Mathew 6:34.

Florida on Fire

The burning of woods in northern Florida, described by Stowe in this article, continues to this day. It was already an old custom when she described it more than a hundred and thirty years ago.[1]

Florida just now is going through the annual burning. It is a practice of great antiquity in this State to burn it over every spring by setting fire to the long, dry grass in order that the fresh young vegetation may spring up in its stead. To a person with a Northern eye and Northern habits of thought this seems a stupid custom, but there is something to say for it. Florida has always been held as a grazing State.[2] Cattle require no shelter or protection from cold during the mild winter and consequently roam in free flocks through the forest. The grass of the woods has a long tough blade, and is aptly named after wire. By the middle of winter this rough grass has become so utterly harsh and tasteless as to afford no nourishment to the half-starved cattle and then their owners proceed to set it on fire. The flame once kindled runs rapidly over the surface of the ground, taking bushes and palmetto trees in its way, licking up the violets, primroses and meadow grasses, sometimes kindling the resinous pine trees which burn like a torch.[3] For a week or two past the horizon has been red here and there with the light of these fires. Yesterday in driving out through the pinewoods we were repeatedly obliged to double and turn to avoid driving directly through them. The brilliant red bands of flame, with their long wavering tongues of light, were sparkling every way with joyous alacrity. Here and there a tall pine tree, with its waving green top, presented a curious spectacle. A hollow place in the trunk had let in the fire to the resinous heart of the tree, and it was all aflame like a fire-place, pouring out blaze and smoke.

A tall green tree, with its heart burning itself out, was a spectacle for Hawthorne's allegorical sight.[4] How long may a man stand waving in [the] air the foliage of a good profession [profusion], while the fires of hell are burning out his heart?[5] Here and there along the ground fallen pine trees were a line of bickering flame, and old pine stumps were blazing like great torches. Through all this our little horse wended his way with the calmness and philosophy of a true Florida pony brought up on the St. Augustine marshes, and accustomed to such things from his infancy.[6] A genuine son of the soil is our Pompey: with never a shoe on his little hoof, he fears nothing in the line of Florida travel. Through palmetto brush, through tangled underbrush, through swollen fords where the water is up to the carriage bottom, Pompey thuds his steady way, looking neither to right nor left, as now he walks between the crackling tongues of flame.

We in Florida have been celebrating Washington's birthday by holding our first State fair. We may have something yet to learn of you Northern folk in the matter of detail and arrangement, but I venture to say no other State in the Union will ever have such a list of productions to exhibit.

There were cabbages of vast circumference; there were enormous turnips, and new potatoes, and sweet potatoes, and peas, and cucumbers, and strawberries, and tomatoes, and squashes, all grown in the open air, and there were cocoanuts hanging in clusters from their stalks just as they grew, and date blossoms and ripe dates on the stalk, pineapples in every stage of growth from the earliest to the latest; ginger root as it grows, leaves and all; custard apple [pawpaw], sugar apple, sapadillo [sapodilla], guavas and pomegranates.[7] Then there were boughs hung with oranges and decked with orange blossoms at the same time. There were the varieties of orange—the little Tangierine [tangerine], with its thin spicy skin and delicate quarters, that might be dissected without spoiling a kid glove; there were blood oranges; there were oranges of enormous size, and lemons no less remarkable; there were citrons, and limes—in short, the whole citrus family was abundantly represented.[8]

In another department were shown preserves of all kinds, oranges preserved whole, limes, and lemons; in various confections, orange marmalade, and citron prepared after the best manner of commerce.

We were also much interested in the specimens of choice poultry. In this fine climate it seems to us that the better varieties of fowl attain to finer size and plumage than elsewhere. Certainly the specimens exhibited were of rare beauty. The only trouble about having such poultry would be that they are absolutely too good to be eaten. We shouldn't sleep for a month if such a cock and hen as we saw exhibited there were slaughtered for us and made to subserve the vulgar purposes of appetite; and such a yard of fowls as we there saw exhibited would be only good to be looked at.

Some of the industrial work of the ladies was quite interesting. There were bed quilts whose piecing and quilting rose towards the domains of a fine art. There was Spanish embroidery, lace work, fine embroidery in worsted done in the choicest manner. What was more interesting—hear this, ye girls that are at ease!—there was a Southern bride's wedding-dress, in war times, spun and woven and made-up by her own fair hands. There's a girl worth having! A girl, we will venture to say, who never has proved, and never will prove, unequal to any exigency. Come, now, girls of the North, who of you can go beyond that?

In the centre of the exhibition was the flower and plant-stand, and the central point of that was a pyramid of three hundred varieties of flowers blooming in the open air on the 22^{d} of February. It was something to gladden the shade of Washington, even from the land

"Where everlasting spring abides."[9]

Curiously, also, there was exhibited a little orange tree in blossom, only one year from the seed. Let nobody publish [purchase] a puff of land in Florida, now, on the strength of this one fact, asserting that oranges usually blossom the first year they are out of the ground. Any calculations of income based on such facts will come to grief, as we fear many too sanguine calculators of life in Florida do.

Now, in closing, one word. We have received a letter from a man in Canada, saying he and many others want to come to Florida, and asking, "Is land plenty, and at what price? And can workingmen find employment? etc., etc. In reply we say land is certainly plenty at all sorts of prices, from $1 to $50 per acre. There is Government land that may be had merely for the occupancy and complying with conditions. But no man or body of men ought to move families to Florida without a personal examination of the ground. If a company of workingmen of small means wish to come to Florida, let them send one of their number to New York, who can there take a schooner bound for Florida and get there at small expense. Arrived at Jacksonville, let him inquire for Solon Robinson, who will put him in the way of finding out all he needs to know.[10]

Good, industrious workingmen, able to rough it, to live cheaply, and work steadily, do seem to do well in our neighborhood. House-carpenters, blacksmiths, and masons have a still better chance. In short, there is no State where skill and industry are better appreciated and likely to be better rewarded in the end than Florida.

Notes

1. This article appeared as "Letter from Florida, Out of the Fire," in the *Christian Union*, March 15, 1876.
2. Grazing State: Crackers in Florida derived much of their income by raising cattle. It was common for them to sell livestock to Cubans in the nineteenth century and, since this trade was based upon gold, many Crackers preferred to sell beef to the Spanish rather than the Confederacy. The cattle industry remains a significant part of Florida's agricultural economy.
3. Primrose: one of the first blooming wildflowers. Primroses are common in fields. They have elongated narrow leaves.
4. Hawthorne's allegorical insight: Nathaniel Hawthorne, American novelist and short story writer.
5. How long may a man stand waving in [the] air the foliage of a good profession [profusion], while the fires of hell are burning out his heart?: not identified.
6. Little horse: for hundreds of years small wild horses, Marsh Tacky, lived on the Sea Islands of the Atlantic coast. Pompey was such a horse.

7. Sugar apple: a tropical fruit related to the custard apple; sapodilla [sapodilla]: a tropical fruit native to southern Mexico and Central America; guavas: a small tropical tree that produces a pink or yellow fruit.
8. Kid gloves: a dress glove made of soft leather; blood oranges: a type of cultivated sweet orange with an unusual red pulp.
9. "Where everlasting spring abides": part of the Isaac Watts hymn "There is a Land of Pure Delight."
10. Solon Robinson: the well-known *New York Tribune* reporter lived in Jacksonville. Knowledgeable of the local economy, he could have been an invaluable resource to any new resident. Given Robinson's infuriating interaction with Stowe, the novelist would not have objected to the reporter being tormented by settlers and tourists. See chapter four.

An Enchanted Evening and a Perfect Day

It has been easy for writers to object to Harriet Beecher Stowe's use of stereotypes, especially that of the good Christian servant in her famous novel—the ever-loyal Uncle Tom. This becomes even truer when little effort is made to place her language and depictions in the context of the era or to compare her writings to those of others in the nineteenth century. Samuel Clemens—Mark Twain—used the "n" word in his novels while obviously not demeaning the African American slave Jim. In Huckleberry Finn *the character that shows the least thought, care, and judgment is not an African American, but Tom Sawyer. The same is true for the writings of educator Samuel Chapman Armstrong. Even though Armstrong established one of the nation's leading colleges for African Americans, Hampton Institute, he used both the "n" word and referred, at times, to his students as "darkies." To dismiss Armstrong as a bigot would be to demean his efforts to produce thousands of black educators.*

In this article Stowe combines now-offensive imagery with profound hope for her subject. She describes an elderly black woman as a "mammy." Stowe seems oblivious to any possible joy or beauty or richness of life the woman may have experienced. She then compares her to a worm. Just as the comparison is made, Stowe instantly hopes the former slave will receive the most amazing blessings that God can grant. She wants the poor and oppressed liberated eternally. The novelist, whatever her faults, rises to genuine inspiration.[1]

March! In almost every quarter of the world a sound of dread, suggestive of fierce winds, blue noses, rain, sleet, slush, snow, hail, and whatever other sign of ill-temper the conflict of earth and air may inaugurate.

But March in Florida is simply altogether lovely. It is the month of serene skies, neither hot nor cold, of soft breezes, of unclouded days, and sun and moon without a veil.

This last week we have had in our settlement a croquet party, given in the open air, by moonlight.[2] To be sure, large fatwood bonfires at the four angles of the lawn helped to define the wickets, as well as to light up the long gray festoons of moss in the old oak hammock, and to give a picturesque brightness to the players on the three croquet grounds as they hurried hither and thither in the excitement of that absorbing game. Hot coffee, carried about from time to time among the players, offered reinforcement of their energies, while those that did not play overlooked the scene from the wide verandas or sat grouped around the flickering bonfires. It was a novel and picturesque scene, and from the pier extending far down into the river we could see the bonfires, the lighted house and passing forms reflected in the river, which was still and waveless as a looking-glass.

But one of the loveliest things now is to wake at midnight when the moon is at her height and hear the mocking-birds singing from the high towers at the top of the live oaks. They trill and warble and go through roulades and execute cadenzas that would be the despair of the prima donna.[3]

Meanwhile, all is fixed and silent besides, the stars look down large and clear through the deep, purplish blue of the sky, and the shadowy veils and draperies of the gray moss scarcely move in the breeze.

African American men, women, and children in Mandarin, Florida, 1880s. State Library and Archive of Florida.

In the daytime there is a great temptation just to sit and do nothing on the front veranda, watching the butterflies. The air at times seems full of them, as if it had suddenly burst into blossoms. They fly in couples, two together circling round each other in and out of the blossoming orange trees, then down in the lowland, where the green feathers of the cypress are now in their most brilliant coloring. It must be a lovely life, this of the butterfly! Supposing sunshine and calm and mild weather to be eternal, it is charming to think of these winged flowers, flitting from place to place—"embodied joys."[4] They have no reflective faculties to trouble them—they are a bright-winged sensation, and nothing more.

The old mythology made the butterfly an emblem of the soul. The comparison is apt. Some of the brightest come from nauseous worms crawling on ever so many filthy legs, a sight of fear and disgust. Then they die and go into a cocoon, which looks for all the world just like a coffin, and by-and-by there is a great bursting of bonds, and out comes this gorgeous and glorious creature, the perfected butterfly. If he remembers his worm-life and the time when his days were one low, vile crawl, what must be his sensations now that he is made a free citizen of the air! There is a fantastic joyousness, a dancing fullness of life, as they go up, up, up into the very topmost branches of the oranges trees, as if they said to each other, "Isn't this delightful! Only think how we used to crawl and labor down there at the roots of things! Who would have thought we were coming to this?"

Well, there is in our neighborhood a poor old black mammy, worn out, with hard usage put upon her through years of slavery, bent with rheumatism, ignorant, hardly able to speak enough English to make herself understood, but kindly, harmless, and well meaning. She has a confused faith in Jesus as a kind Master who will by-and-by do something for her. Well, by-and-by to her, as to us all, will come the chrysalis state, the coffined rest, and then the new life-bright, strange, winged—the splendid butterfly out of the dark, repulsive worm. We have sometimes looked at these butterflies and hoped that they shadowed out [foreshadow] the joys the Father has in store for many a poor worn-out seamstress or washerwoman, many a barren, confined, undeveloped nature whose life here has been toil and hardship. To them shall come the winged life, the free air, the exultation of liberty, rest, beauty, forever. Let us hope it; all things are possible with God.

Birds! The air is full of them! The jays, loud, obtrusive, noisy, never letting you alone a minute; the red bird, singing, obtrusively, "What cheer! What cheer! What cheer," and the mocking bird that listens and mocks and echoes all the rest, weaving their songs in snatches and bits into his own pot pourri of music, and then the host of anonymous chirpers and twitterers who keep the air every moment full of sound.

We are interested in brown thrashers.[5] We never knew why they are called so, but think we have found out: they are called thrashers because they thrash. This little fellow now before us in front of our verandah has an acorn which he is pounding and thrashing with his beak, putting his whole soul into the work. Birds work for their living. There is no mistake of that. This Mr. Thrasher, who inhabits our front yard, is a bird of energy, and the top of his bill is a very decided one. Then there are the butcher birds, who have notions of their own about cookery, and so impale their prey on the long orange thorns till the sun cooks it to their taste.[6] We find unfortunate grasshoppers and beetles thus spitted in our walks through the neighborhood. Blue birds are plenty here. They fly in flocks, and their brilliant plumages make quite a feature in the landscape.

Birds are one step higher in creation than butterflies, in as much as they have a voice in addition to their wings. The butterflies ought to sing to make their being complete, but they seem to have neither voice nor ear. You never see a butterfly listening to the mocking bird; he lives in a different world, and perhaps has no ears to hear with.

It is today as near as possible perfect weather. The breeze comes over from the ocean, and tempers what would else be the too great heat of the sun, which even now wilts the young, tender leaves where it falls upon them directly.

It is a day to sit and look far off over blue waters to distant shores, to watch white moving sails, to speculate dreamily and to wonder if there can be such a dust and fuss and clamor and commotion as the newspapers tell us is going on in the great world. Oh, poor, poor world! Oh, noisy voices! Oh, men and women who spend your money for that which is not bread! Is there not something better and higher for us all than this dusty medley of wrangle and toil and shrieks? Surely there is: nature in its sweetness and beauty, its calm and glory; birds with their wings and songs, butterflies rising from lowest to highest forms, teach us there is a better life to be lived, and higher hopes. By and by we shall all be gone—all the accusers and accused; all the strivers, all the contending, clamoring voices; every one, all alone, each by himself, will have gone through the last death struggle and been laid away in his separate grave.[7]

1876—this Centennial Year! what noise, what commotion![8] But before 1976—what stillness! Yes, we can all of us look at that date and know that long before that time we shall know certainly what is beyond the veil. Those who have put all their hopes on the Word of Jesus will have known in whom they believed. Before 1976 we shall have seen the King in his beauty, and shall be dwellers in the land that is now far away.

Notes

1. Stowe published this article as "Croquet, Butterflies, Birds, Sunshine and Moonlight in Florida," *Christian Union*, March 29, 1876.
2. Croquet: a yard game with wooden balls and mallets. The balls are driven through metal hoops or wickets.
3. Roulades: vocal embellishments sung to a single note.
4. Embodied joys: perhaps a reference to Zephaniah 3:14-17.
5. Thrasher: a relative of the mockingbird with longer tail and a curved beak.
6. Butcher bird: a shrike. These gray or brown birds eat insects often after impaling them on thorns.
7. Accusers and the accused: this surely must allude to one of the sensational trials of the era which occurred after Stowe's famous brother, Henry Ward Beecher, was sued for adultery.
8. What commotion: both the centennial and bicentennial were accompanied with elaborate celebrations.

Modern Florida Envisioned

Growth in tourism occurred in the years before the nation's centennial. At the centennial a number of writers speculated about the future of the nation—an interest that was encouraged by new technology. A Scientific American *in 1877, for instance, announced successful communications on a telephone. Charles Beecher used the opportunity to project Florida's future to the bicentennial—when the entire state had a population, as one writer put it, "half the size of West Virginia's in the same period."[1] Beecher foresaw vast development. He assumed that air travel would become common, letting Yankees commute to winter homes in Florida. In his musing here, Charles Beecher combines the fantastic and the fanciful with the prophetic.[2]*

SPANISH HOLE HOTEL

Wakulla Co., Fla.,[3] 1976

Dear George: From your hyperborean hights [*sic*] on the straits of Belle Isle, if the blending [*sic*] snow storms will let you, look down upon us in this wave girdled pavilion.[4] Much as we have traveled, and familiar as we are with hotel life in every land, we here enjoy a new experience. Conceive of an immense edifice erected on piles driven, or screwed rather, deep into the bottom, so that the waves can freely dash between and under the floor of the lower story! This is owing to the tidal waves that sometimes set in from the Gulf in a southerly gale, rising to a hight of ten feet or more. No structure, however firm, could stand the shock of the billows [waves]; but between these piles they rush harmless. All the wharves, docks, railways, warehouses, public, and private buildings are constructed in the same manner, so that it is like another Venice, a city of the sea. Long, wide streets without a foot of terra firma, or a tree; traversed by innumerable small craft, among which is the recently introduced gondola. No wonder a place so unique in its character should be thronged with gay visitors from every part of the world.

We arrived here last night from Key West, having completed the circuit of the flowery State by the Rim Road. What a capital name for a railroad! It might have been called the tire road, by a sort of *lucus a non lercendo,* because it never tires you; and because it binds the State as a tire binds the wheel.[5] But rim is better, the whole Floridian peninsula being girt with a rim of flashing steel.

We left our friends, the A's, at Jacksonville, and stopped for a day or two at several of the chief cities on our route, especially New Smyrna and Miami.[6] At the latter we debated whether we would visit the Nobles and other Canadian friends now residing at Everglades, a beautiful section once covered with water, but now, since the completion of the grand Southern Peninsula drainage works, a paradise, and one of the most densely peopled portions of the State.

We concluded, however, to go round on the Rim and afterwards pay them a flying visit, via the new Ærial line, just opened in opposition to the old Air Ship line whose rates have been latterly considered rather exorbitant. So after a few delightful days on Biscayne waters, and sundry excursions in the environs, we sped southward to Key West.

Here we were welcomed by the Kings, the Everetts and Coltons, old friends and old settlers here. It is about half a century, I think, since they left the prairies. You may judge of the healthfulness of the region from the fact that the physicians are all immensely wealthy, yet men of leisure. The system now-a-days is for a few families to pay a physician a regular annual salary, say of a dollar per diem, for each well day in the year; deducting ten dollars per die for every sick day. On the ancient system the more sickness the wea ier the physician. Now the reverse is true. In fact funerals are grow g obsolete, and death is dying out.

Delicious climate! What roses! What fruits! Why shoul ven a saint wish to die or be translated [transported] from such a ven on earth as this!

We were looking the other day in the Key West Athena Library at the Antiquarian Collections.[7] Among other things chanced on an old atlas of 1876. What curious ideas the world had o geography then! Yet what a fuss they made in that Centennial, about their progress in knowledge! Well, by that atlas it seems Key West was at that time an island, and not as now connected with the main land. The formation of the Sahara Sea has doubtless contributed to the emergence of the Peninsula, though some attribute it in part to Volcanic causes.

While here, Azalea Colton arrived in one of her father's vessels from Canton, via the Panama Canal across the Isthmus of Darien.[8] She is much improved, and quite proud of her voyage round the world. New York, Liverpool, Suez Canal, Canton, Darien, Key West, home.

As it happened an adorer of hers, M. Alphonse, arrived here about the same time from Algeria. He has charge of the immense salt works of the French Government. The evaporation of the equatorial sea is such that the surplus population of Africa find steady employment in collecting saline deposits along the coast, and in the government's dredging works. Hence the disappearance of the slave trade immediately after the Sea was opened and the native tribes put on regular wages.

Scientific men were apprehensive before the enterprise was a success, that a sea so shallow would soon evaporate, and leave a desert of salt, instead of sand. But Alphonse says that all fears of such a result have long since ceased to be entertained. On the contrary, while the world is supplied with excellent salt, to the enrichment of the French Empire, the sea is kept at an average depth of eighty feet, and the continent redeemed from malaria and slavery.

You would h ve been interested had you been present at the President's recep n the other evening, for in these days of aerial voyages, great en are not confined to the metropolis, and courts and cabinets ubiquitous, many of the magnates of the general government h ng semi-tropical winter residences.

Am g other distinguished guests, besides the chief official of this Sta conversed with Don Miguel, U.S. Senator from Mexico and Se Llanos, M. C. from Cuba. He gave me a most interesting nt of the World's Collection of Antiquities in the Havana Har. Since the disarmament of Nations the ironclads and other war essels of all nations (such as have not rotted away) are collected here and carefully preserved for the inspection of mankind. What enormous waste of brain-power and of cash are those ponderous old things! No wonder the world was poor and the nations bankrupt! But as soon as armies and navies were voted down, the nations paid their debts in a hurry. Señor Llanos said he did not know which affected him most strangely, to stand in Agassiz's museum with Mastodons and Ichthyosauri and other Paleontological forms, or to go inside the revolving turrets of these horrid iron monsters with their grim engines of destruction.[9]

While we were conversing Don Miguel joined us, saying he could not tell which had contributed most to the general health and wealth of mankind, the abolition of war, or the discovery of the cause and specific cure of malarial complaints. Fevers, once the bane of hot countries (though by no means confined to them) being now unknown, the greatest drawback to social progress seems removed.

While we old folks thus discussed grave subjects, the young folks were not idle. Brightest and gayest of the glittering throng you might have seen fair Azalea, and her lover, I suppose we may now call him. I saw him whispering earnestly in her ear in the conservatory something at which she blushed like fire, and then grew pale; but said never a word, save with her eyes, but that look Alphonse seemed at no loss to interpret, for as it led her to join the dances, he seemed treading on air.

Oh the new world, how bright and beautiful it is! Everywhere prosperity, progress, success and "Sorrow shall come again no more."

The day after the reception we resumed our journey on the sumptuous Rim Road palace car and stopping over a day each at Charlotte Harbor, Manatee, Tampa, Cedar Key, arrived at this Pavilion of the Gulf, or as some call it, Pavilion of the Volcano, where we propose to abide several days.

Men now living have in early life conversed with those who could remember when this coast, and in fact the whole State was all a wilderness. No air lines; no railroads, no Ocean and Gulf Canal; no Volcano.[10] Among other curiosities in the Museum of Antiquities at Key West that I told you of, I came across some numbers of a paper, once notorious, the *New York Herald* in which were letters from this very region. A staff correspondent weltering through swamps hunting for a Volcano; nailing sticks upon high pine trees, and finding nothing after all.

If it had not been for the Canal almost running the Volcano down as you may say, perhaps we never should have found it.

Hereafter I must tell you about my visit to some of the marvels of this county of mystery, for such I am told is the meaning of the word Wakulla.[11] Adieu, faithfully thine,

Charles Beecher

P.S.—A monster tow of grain barges has just arrived at St. Marks from Montana. I was up there and saw the great sturdy boatmen, fresh from their icy heights, and bringing a whiff of winter as it were with them. How like a miracle it seems to them here! In a few days thousands of bushels of grain laid down on the Atlantic coast for world distribution! [C. B.]

Notes

1. Half the size … same period: Grunwald, *The Swamp*, 73.
2. Originally published as "Florida a Hundred Years Hence" in the *Semi-Tropical*, July 1877.
3. A fictional place.
4. Belle Isle: the channel between Labrador and Newfoundland in Canada.
5. *Lucus a non lecendo:* a far-fetched explanation that is not correct, to name something after something it is not.

6. Miami: to predict that Miami would be a "chief city" in the 1870s was remarkable when you consider that it had a population of 1,681 people in 1900.
7. Athenaeum Library: for this fictitious institution Charles Beecher modifies the name of a Boston library.
8. Darien: French did not start work on their ill-fated effort to build a Panama Canal until January 1882.
9. Agassiz's museum: a prominent Swiss scientist, Louis Agassiz, founded the Museum of Comparative Zoology at Harvard University in 1859.
10. Volcano: The supposed source of a plume of smoke commonly seen in Wakulla County. This is a reference to a mysterious plume of smoke on the skyline above Wakulla County. Its presence led to public interest and an extensive search. In 1886 an earthquake centered in South Carolina was felt even in Tallahassee. After this event, the smoke from the "volcano" was never seen again.
11. Wakulla: name may refer to "mysterious waters."

Protect the Birds

Of the articles Harriet Beecher Stowe wrote about Florida after Palmetto-Leaves, *this is the best known.*[1] *During Stowe's numerous travels by steamboat in Florida, she had watched male tourists shoot wildlife for their idle amusement. On an excursion up Julington Creek in* Palmetto-Leaves, *she described a fish-hawk, "he is a bird of no mean size and proportions—[and he] has as good right to think that the river and the fish were made for him as we..." After adding more details about the bird, Stowe rejoiced at the absence of wanton destruction: "Thankful are we that no mighty hunter is aboard, and that the atrocity of shooting a bird on her nest will not be perpetrated here. We are a harmless company, and mean so well by them..."*[2]

While Stowe continued to register her disgust in other articles in the Christian Union, *especially on her journey up the Ocklawaha River to Silver Springs, she had an additional incentive for writing this article. In the period of the nation's centennial, Charles Beecher projected the growth of modern Florida to the bicentennial.*[3] *Besides predicting a population in the millions, he believed that development would overwhelm the Everglades. The famous habitat would cease to exist. Stowe, having endlessly promoted Florida, now saw where the process would lead. With this awareness, the famous novelist sought legal protection for birds and, perhaps to her surprise, the state's legislature actually passed a law.*

The editors of this present book brought public attention to "Protect the Birds" when they wrote about the birth of modern Florida in Beechers, Stowes, and Yankee Strangers. *Realizing the article's enduring significance, they published it in its entirety in the second printing of their book.*[4] *Later, Michael Grunwald, when he traced the destruction of wildlife in his* The Swamp: The Everglades, Florida, and the Politics of Paradise *(2006), cited Stowe's article, and used its title for the title of his own eighth chapter.*[5] *There is awareness among environmentalists of "Protect the Birds" and Stowe's insights.*

The Legislature of Florida meets in January, and cannot *The Semi-Tropical* rouse some one to present before them the claims of the birds of Florida to protection[?]

Florida has been considered in all respects as a prey and a spoil to all comers. Its splendid flowers and trees, its rare and curious animals have been looked upon as made and created only to please the fancy of tourists—to be used and abused as the whims of the hour might dictate. Thousands of idle loungers pour down here every year, people without a home or landed interest in the State, and whose only object seems to be to amuse themselves while in it without the least consideration of future results to the country.

The decks of boats are crowded with men, whose only feeling amid our magnificent forests, seems to be a wild desire to shoot something, and who fire at every living thing on shore, careless of maiming, wounding or killing the living creatures which they see, full of life and enjoyment. Were they hunters expecting profit of any kind from the game, there might be apology and defense for this course. But to shoot for the mere love of killing is perfect barbarism, unworthy of any civilized man, and, unless some protection shall be extended over the animal creation, there is danger that there may be a war of extermination waged on our forests.

Besides the guns of hunters, the birds of Florida are exposed to the incursions of bird trappers, who come regularly every year and trap and carry off by thousand, and tens of thousands the bright children of our forests. These birds die by hundreds in passage to New York and Europe. It is a perfect slave trade [all] over again, and it is slowly and surely robbing our beautiful State of one of its chief attractions.

The number of red birds, mocking birds, and nonpareils has very sensibly diminished in Duval county within the last five years.[6] That which used to be a constant source of pleasure and delight in their song and plumage is becoming a rarity, and if things go on many years more as they have done, it will cease altogether.

There may be those who will have little care for this. There are those who care nothing for beauty or for song—but who are dead set, only and fully on something to eat. They accuse the birds of stealing their peas and grapes, and declare that they would be glad to see them exterminated.

Have they ever reflected, what else birds eat besides peas and grapes? Have they reflected that they are all the while searching the ground for insects—for the eggs and larvae of what will become destructive to vegetation? The bird eats a pea, to be sure, for his salad, but he takes a dozen cut-worms for his meat.[7] Guided by unerring instinct they pick the corn worm from its green shell—they find the burrows and holes where the eggs of destructive insects hide and pick them out.

Now, in the cold Northern States where the winter freezes the noxious insects and keeps down their increase, still the value of birds as guardians against their ravages is so well known, that protective laws exist in most of the Northern States, to prevent the reckless destruction of the feathered tribes.

How much more do we need bird help in the hot, teeming soil of Florida, where the ground never freezes and where insect life swarms in every direction. We had better pay the taxes of a few peas and grapes and have the birds for under gardeners, than to suffer as some of the Western States are now suffering by losing crop after crop through grasshoppers.

An army of mocking birds would soon make an end of grasshoppers. These light guerrilla warriors, feathered and mailed, are God's own police, meant to search out and keep down the noxious abundance of animal life, where the dull eye of man cannot see and the slow foot of man cannot tread. Those bright, quick eyes and buoyant wings, go up and down searching, picking, devouring.

Florida is now setting out thousands of orange groves, and, if nothing happens, may have a harvest golden as the Hesperides.[8] But what if the orange insect comes down upon us as the grasshoppers have in the West? Is it not safer to protect the birds?

Who, now, will appear for the birds? Who will get a protection law passed that will secure to us the song, the beauty, and the usefulness of these charming fellow citizens of our lovely Florida?

Notes

1. Published with this title in *Semi-Tropical*, January 1877.
2. H. B. Stowe, *Palmetto-Leaves*, 77, 78.
3. Charles Beecher, "Florida a Hundred Years Hence," *Semi-Tropical*, July 1877. The article appears in chapter 13 of this book.
4. "Protect the Birds" appears on pages xx-xxii in the second printing of Foster and Foster's *Beechers, Stowes, and Yankee Strangers*.
5. The chapter "Protect the Birds" starts on page 117.
6. Nonpareils: the painted bunting. Its many colors make it one of the most striking birds in North American.
7. Cut-worms: mouth larva which eats the roots of plants and can cut the stem off at the ground.
8. Hesperides: the mythological garden where golden apples grew.

Almost an Ending

Harriet Beecher Stowe, like other major authors—especially Samuel Clemens—began going on lecture tours. In the 1870s, this became a source of revenue for her family and by the end of the decade the novelist's efforts in writing declined. Stowe published no novels after Poganuc People *in 1878. As a noted biographer put it, this "marked the end of the literary career she had begun forty-four years earlier." While this is true, the novelist did write about Florida a few more times. The following article is among her last.*[1] *It seems very humorous—a wonderful aspect of Stowe's personality.*[2]

"Now, auntie, can't you tell me a Florida story?" said little Tom, seating himself down by me, and looking up with eyes of expectation.

Florida is supposed by everyone to be a sort of land of "myths and marvels"—and why shouldn't stories in any quantity be forthcoming from one who has spent the half of twelve years there?

"Well, Tom," said I,—searching back in memory,—"I'll tell you an Indian story that was told to me by an old gentleman, of what happened to him once in the time of the Florida War [First and Second Seminole Wars].

"And first I must begin by telling you a little about what the Florida War was about.

"You will see if you look at a map that the State of Georgia joins right on to Florida at the North. Now in the old times the slaves in Georgia used to run away and go to the Indians in Florida. The Indians were kind to them, and received and protected them, and finally so many ran away that the Georgians petitioned the United States Government to send an army down into Florida to fight the Indians and get back their slaves.

"This was what caused the Florida War, and it lasted seven years and cost the lives of a great many brave men.

"For, you see, the Indians, who were used to living in swamps and forests, and knew all about the wild cats and the panthers and the moccasin snakes, and the rattlesnakes, had altogether the advantage of the poor fellows that were sent down into the wild country and didn't know anything about these things.

"The Indians had learned how to use guns from the white men, and they would often sit quite at their ease up in the trees and pick off soldiers who were floundering and struggling through swamps and thickets below.

"Well, the old gentleman that told me the story was captain of a small schooner that used to run up and down the St. Johns River. He said that once he was hired by [the] Government to take some arms and ammunition up a long crooked river to a fort which had been established out in the wild woods.

"They had on board a cannon and some other arms and ever so many balls and some casks of powder for the use of the men in the fort.

"Well, he said it was pretty slow work, for the river ran through deep tangled forests, where the trees and branches would meet overhead and as they pushed their way through, sometimes the black, poisonous moccasin snakes would drop from the branches upon the boat.

"You see, the moccasin has a fashion of coming out of the water to air himself on logs—or branches of trees—in fact.

"I once heard of a man who went bathing in one of the streams and hung his clothes over a low branch, and when he came back from swimming, he found a colony of black moccasin snakes established upon them as comfortably as possible, and it took some time and a good many sticks and stones to get them to decamp and let him have his clothes again.

"Well, this Capt. Smith said that they pushed and pulled and rowed up this crooked river, sometimes catching a little breeze, but oftener obliged to use poles and the oars, and making but slow progress.

"At last they were within half a mile of the fort, that is to say, if they could have walked there directly, the distance was no more than this, but as the river made a great bend there, it would be two or three miles before the schooner would arrive at the fort.

"It was in the afternoon of a hot day, and as they were near the fort, they were taking matters quite easily, and were settling themselves to have an after-dinner nap, when suddenly a great tall Indian in war-paint and with a necklace of bear's claws and rattlesnakes' tails round his neck stepped out of a palmetto thicket and walked quietly on board the schooner; right behind him came another, and right behind him another and others, till there were fourteen great strong fellows, hideously painted.

"They all stopped on board the schooner and sat down without speaking a word.

"The moment the captain saw their war-paint he knew the lives of himself and his crew were at their mercy.

"There were only three or four hands on the schooner. They had no protection against the Indians.

"There was something quite awful in the silent way the creatures sat there, having taken possession of the little schooner.

"They uttered no word or sound, but solemnly looked down like so many statues.

"The captain was turning over in his own mind what he should do. There was no use in trying to run, for the Indians could outrun any white man.

"At last he recognized, under all the disguise of war-paint and feathers, an Indian that he had had some former acquaintance with, and that could speak English.

"He began to talk with him.

"What were they going to do with them? he inquired.

"He was told that they were to be kept till moonrise that night, and then be offered up as a sacrifice.

"Now the captain knew something about these terrible sacrifices in which captives were slowly consumed with fire, and he drew a deep breath.

"His Indian acquaintance, seeing his feelings, said in a conciliatory tone,—

"'Well, no mind—me kill you myself—me no let hurt you.'

"The captain found very little consolation even in the thought of being killed outright when his companions lingered in horrible tortures, and he set his wits to work to open some communication with their friends in the fort.

"After a while the Indians began to survey the schooner, and look over the things in it with some appearance of interest, as booty which belonged to them.

"The cannon seemed to excite their curiosity; they examined over and under and around; looked in at the muzzle, and conversed with each other about it.

"The captain, through the interpreter, explained its uses, and offered to show a specimen of its power, to which they all agreed with an appearance of great curiosity.

"So, charging it with a very heavy charge of ball, chains, nails, and whatever would cut its way through the woods, he fired it off—and cut a cracking path through the forest towards the fort with a tremendous reverberation.

"The Indians, some of whom fell over at the sound, but immediately recovering, laughed, danced, and shouted, and insisted on having the thing done again; and the captain, you may believe, was in no way unwilling to oblige them.

"He loaded up the gun a second time and touched it off again, and this time had the pleasure of hearing a discharge from the fort in reply; so he loaded and fired again and again.

"It was not long before a troop of horse[s] was seen cantering through the bushes, and rifle bullets began to whistle about the heads of the Indians.

"With one deep exclamation, 'Ugh!' the leader plunged into the palmetto thicket, and all the rest after him, and by the time the company of horse arrived at the schooner, there was not one Indian in sight.

"The schooner forthwith was started on her way with a troop of horsemen keeping her in sight along the shore, and before the moonrise the captain and his charge were safe inside the fort.

"Right glad were they to be there, too, as you may well believe."

"What became of the Indians?" asked Tom, for whom a story was never long enough.

"Oh, as to the Indians, the troops knew too much to try to chase them through the woods and swamps; they were glad enough to have them take themselves off.

"The captain lived to be an old man and to tell the story long after the Indians wars were over."

Notes

1. This article originally appeared as "A Story of Florida" in *Youth's Companion,* June 2, 1881.
2. Joan Hedrick, *Harriet Beecher Stowe: A Life,* 392.

Harriet Beecher Stowe in 1853. State Library and Archive of Florida.

Harriet Beecher Stowe and Florida Today

Within Stowe's publications about Florida are thoughts that are relevant to issues of our time. Years before she sought legislation in "Protect the Birds," she wrote a statement with wider implications.[1] She would not have hesitated to expand laws to protect other forms of wildlife:

> Alas, there is only one sorrow, one blot on the pleasure [of boating on the Ocklawaha River]. The slaughter of the innocents! On the deck of the boat are men who see no beauty in nature, who have no sympathy with the wild, free, lovely life of the forest, and whose only aim is to leave a bullet in every palpitating living creature they pass. The shrieks of poor, wounded water birds, who first learn the dire secret of pain, the lingering agonies of maimed, helpless creatures, crawling away to die, unpitied. Such are the traces man leaves in God's untroddened Eden.
>
> What makes the thing more inexcusable is, that there is no pretense of game. Nothing shot is taken, or pretended to be taken, and half of the men are bad marksmen, that can only mutilate. Surely the Christian religion ought to have taught men at least as much tenderness for animals as

> was shown by the laws of Moses thousands of years ago. If not a sparrow falls without the Father's feeling it, what must the loving God think of such scenes as every boat in these lovely forests witness?

Stowe celebrated Florida's beauty and frequently compared it to that of Italy, but she knew of the potential cost of development. Having helped to bring thousands of tourists to the state, she was mindful of the price paid for it. Note her description of Mandarin long before many of her Florida promotions had been written:

> We have heard of nothing but snows from you, North Poleites, this season. Well, it is snowing here in another fashion—snowing orange blossoms! The ground is white with the falling showers. They fill the boat, which has been drawn up under the trees to be newly painted. They snow down on Frank's black head; they lie in little whirls and drifts on the flat roof of the kitchen, and are floating about in clouds of perfume through the lazy air. Never was such a blossoming! The trees seem delicious with blossoms—over-blooming—crowding the branches. Fair art thou among trees, oh, lovely orange, queen and bride of trees! We see now why the orange blossom has been sacred to weddings, symbol of sweetness, and fruitfulness, and ever-exuberant life.

A few paragraphs later, Stowe turns to description of Florida's abandoned orange groves and then adds that they are "God's own wild fruit garden":

> For silent years and ages the golden fruit has ripened and fallen, and gone back into soil at the root of these old trees, and been received back into the tree, and come out again in leaves and blossoms. Flocks of green parquets, bands of jays and mocking birds, red birds, and orioles have built, and reared, and sung, and chattered in their shade, and only to-day the tramp of the tourist is beginning to profane the shadows and lay bare the secrets of

> these orange wildernesses.[2] We must confess it seems a pity! Is there nothing that is not to be made common?—nothing that Brown, Jones, and Robinson are not to tramp over and through, carpet-bag in hand, touching, tasting, smelling, and firing guns at every wild and tame thing they see?[3]
>
> These acres of ever-blooming orange trees were a field for the imagination—one might fancy them as belonging to a region beyond the vulgar life of earth; but all that is over now. The Philistines are upon them, and they will be cut up into lots for speculators.[4]

Stowe's fears for these sacred groves were realized. They were sold and in the 1890s the groves were destroyed by two devastating freezes. With these events the citrus industry shifted away. In the same era, much of the development of Florida focused on new resorts along the coast—to places like Palm Beach and then to Miami. The St. Johns River ceased being a magnet for tourists and the real estate developers scurried elsewhere. This did not end environmental destruction. It continued in the hands of farmers, ranchers, and misguided government officials, including those of the Corps of Engineers. Somewhere near the St. Johns, however, there are a few unnoticed orange trees—that sprang up from seeds and roots after bitter weather.

Obviously, Stowe would endorse ecological tourism, seeing immense value in nature that human beings had not touched. Her keen naturalist's eye would not fail to notice an immense cypress tree whose birth predates Poncè de Leon's or the thousands of acres of marshes spilling out of the Timucuan Ecological Preserve.[5] In her wisdom she would also relish nature's wondrous ability to reclaim. If you seek her apparition, look for it in the golden twilight of a spring day. She would have found the forgotten orange trees with their perfect blossoms. The petals drift around her in a breeze as gentle as it is sweet. Florida still offers dreams.

Notes

1. The quotations in this chapter were published as a part of "A Southern Snow-Storm," *Christian Union*, April 16, 1873.
2. Green parquets: a reference to the extinct Carolina parakeets.
3. Robinson: Solon Robinson, the intrusive reporter.
4. The Philistines: a person who trades or sells things without regard for their artistic merit.
5. Timucuan Ecological Preserve: a national park near the mouth of the St. Johns River, east of downtown Jacksonville.

Appendix

A Letter from Stowe's First Trip to Florida: An African American Prayer Meeting

Harriet Beecher Stowe's publications about the Sunshine State began in 1867 and probably ended in 1881. Most of them are listed in Margaret Holbrook Hildreth's bibliography.[1] *While Hildreth's work remains an invaluable contribution to scholars, she admitted readily that it was not exhaustive. She expected that unrecorded works by Stowe existed within newspapers. The following letter from the* New York Herald, *May 4, 1867—an article not named by Holbrook—confirms this belief. The* Herald, *by the way, simply reprinted it from the* Boston Watchman and Reflector. *It is very likely that more Florida materials will be discovered as more nineteenth century newspapers are put online. This is especially true from 1867 to 1869, when Stowe did not edit* Hearth and Home.

Forgotten Stowe articles can also be found in a different type of publication. Hildreth did not realize the existence of a periodical based in Florida, The Semi-Tropical. *This monthly publication carried two of Stowe's articles along with several by Charles Beecher. Half of these materials are reprinted in this work, one by each sibling. It also seems possible that state-oriented magazines in other places also carried Stowe works that remain outside Hildreth's knowledge.*

The following published letter came from Stowe's first visit to Florida. Since she arrived in March and it was published in May, it might have been her first article.[2]

On Sunday evening, after our arrival in Jacksonville, we expressed a wish to visit the meeting of the colored people, a thing quite easy to do, as there were two very large, active prayer meetings—the one Baptist and the other Methodist—within a stone's throw of each other on the green which forms a sort of central point in the place [in the town]. We entered and found a very plain but respectable room almost filled with the worshippers, with a pulpit and raised platform at one end. The greater proportion [of the congregation] were the pure, jet black, unmixed Ethiopian—the admixture of lighter tints much less than we have often seen. The women, especially the elder ones, appeared in the characteristic turban, which is so becoming, and were dressed with scrupulous neatness. An ancient negress, attired in her Sunday best, with her high turban, her apron, her neatly crossed handkerchief, has something weird and sibylline in her blackness and gravity, and there were rows of these dark sisters sitting, like solemn birds of augury, on the benches round the pulpit.[3] A black preacher and exhorter occupied the desk in the front of the pulpit, and two grave, white headed old negroes sat above him in the shadow of the dimly lighted pulpit. The exhorter stumbled through a chapter of the Sermon on the Mount—reading painfully and with slow pauses, but with most earnest devotion, and then he exhorted and prayed.[4] After this, Rev. Mr. Kennedy offered a few remarks and a prayer. I noticed that the weird sisters in the turbans paid the most absorbed attention, and when any speaker made a point that struck them, would nod their heads with gravity and murmur, "Dat's so." In the singing, however, everybody seemed to vibrate as if they had all been struck by a musical accord. There was a rhythmical movement of heads, hands, and feet of the whole mass, and it seemed difficult to restrain more responsive actions. We had expressed the desire to hear them sing some of their own peculiar religious melodies in their own way. The fact is, the negroes have two entirely distinct styles of singing; one closely imitated from the white people, which is solemn, dull and nasal, consisting in repeating two lines of a hymn, and then singing it, and then two more, ad infinitum. They use for this sort of worship that one everlasting melody, which may be remembered by all persons familiar with Western and

Southern camp meetings, as applying equally well to long, short or common metre.[5] This style of proceeding they evidently consider the more dignified style of the two, as being a closer imitation of white, genteel worship—having in it about as little soul as most stereotyped religious forms of well instructed congregations. The other style of singing, which they practice when they are by themselves, and which they do because they feel like it, is evidently a traditional descent from that which Mungo Park describes as having heard in Africa years ago.[6] It is sort of [a] union of singing and rhythmic movement, of a solemn and serious character, and conducted with perfect time. The brethren form a ring outside the altar, and the sisters begin to form into a line, while the voice[s] struck up a wild, peculiar air, and the first sister in the female procession shook hands with the first brother, singing the chorus and concluding with a short courtesy [curtsy]; and then, passing on to the next, repeated the same. Soon there was seen a double file of these men and women, moving and singing, and shaking hands and curtseying, all in the most exact time and with the most solemn gravity. The airs were wild and full of spirit—the words simple and often repeated. Some of them I recall:

> We'll camp awhile in de wilderness,
> In de wilderness,
> In de wilderness,
> We'll camp awhile in de wilderness,
> And den we'll all go home.

Or this—

> I want to climb up Jacob's ladder,[7]
> Jacob's ladder,
> Jacob's ladder,
> I want to climb up Jacob's ladder;
> But I cannot do it till I've
> Made my peace wid da Lord.
> Den I'll praise Him,
> Den I'll praise Him—
> I'll praise Him till I die,

And sing Jerusalem.

Some are even more peculiar. There is one beginning—

Who's dat a standing dere?
Who's dat a standing dere?
O, it's General Jesus,
It's General Jesus;
I'll praise Him till I die.

Very soon there was a rhythmical column extending up one aisle, down the other, and slowly moving out of the house at one end. The singing was kept up till every member of the congregation had taken their turn and so passed out. When the fervor was at its height the wild commingling of the voices, the rhythmical movement of turbaned heads, the sense of time and tone that seemed to pervade the whole procession was quite wonderful. All this while the two old preachers sat back in the shadows of the pulpit, black and unmoved as the marble statues of Memphis in Egyptian museums. It was really a most curious sight. The negroes cannot be English or American; they are a fervent tropical growth, best fitted for these warm sunny climes.

Notes

1. Margaret Holbrook Hildreth. *Harriet Beecher Stowe: A Bibliography.*
2. This letter was published as "Letter from Harriet Beecher Stowe on the Negro as He is." *New York Herald*, May 4, 1867. The original is in poor condition. Many words are barely legible.
3. Birds of augury: signs of the will of the gods, ravens.
4. Exhorter: an assistant to the minister who reads scripture and offers advice.
5. Short or common metre: often iambic lines of seven accents arranged in pairs that rhyme.
6. Mungo Park explored the interior of West Africa in the 1790s and just after the beginning of the nineteenth century.
7. Jacob's ladder: a ladder to heaven described by Jacob in his dream at Bethel, Genesis 28:10-13.

Bibliography of Works Cited

Applegate, Debby. *The Most Famous Man in America: The Biography of Henry Ward Beecher*. New York: Doubleday. 2006.

Ash, Stephen V. *Firebrand of Liberty: The Story of Two Black Regiments that Changed the Course of the Civil War*. New York: W. W. Norton, 2006.

Beecher, Charles. "A Century Hence." *Semi-Tropical* 4 (February 1878): 86-87.

_______. "Florida." *Old and New* 1 (February 1870): 178-81.

_______. "Florida a Hundred Years Hence." *Semi-Tropical* 3 (July 1877): 389-91.

Bill, Ledyard. *A Winter in Florida: Or, Observations on the Soil, Climate and Products of our Semi-Tropical State*. New York: Wood and Holbrook, 1869.

Cash, William T. *The Story of Florida*. New York: American Historical Society, 1938.

Chandler, David Leon. *Henry Flagler: The Astonishing Life and Times of the Visionary Robber Baron Who Founded Florida*. New York: Macmillan, 1986.

Davis, T. Frederick. *History of Jacksonville, Florida, and Vicinity, 1513 to 1924.* St. Augustine: The Record Company, 1925.

Foner, Eric. *Reconstruction: America's Unfinished Revolution, 1863-1877.* New York: Harper and Row, 1988.

Foster, John T., Jr., and Sarah Whitmer Foster. *Beechers, Stowes, and Yankee Strangers: The Transformation of Florida.* Gainesville: University Press of Florida, 1999.

_______. "Historic Notes and Documents: Harriet Ward Foote Hawley: Civil War Journalist." *Florida Historical Quarterly* (Spring 2005): 448-67.

_______. "In the Aftermath of the Battle of Olustee: A Beecher's Surprise Visit to Florida." *Florida Historical Quarterly* 86 (Winter 2008): 380-89.

_______. "John Sanford Swaim: A Life at the Beginning of Modern Florida." *Methodist History* 26 (July 1988): 229-40.

_______. "The Last Shall Be First: Northern Methodists in Reconstruction Jacksonville." *Florida Historical Quarterly* 70 (Winter 1992): 265-80.

Foster, John T., Jr., Herbert B. Whitmer, Jr., and Sarah Whitmer Foster. "Tourism Was Not the Only Purpose: Jacksonville Republicans and Newark's Sentinel of

Freedom." *Florida Historical Quarterly* 63 (Winter 1985): 318-24.

Foster, Sarah Whitmer and John T. Foster, Jr. "Chloe Merrick Reed: Freedom's First Lady." *Florida Historical Quarterly* 71 (Winter 1993): 279-99.

Graff, Mary B. *Mandarin on the St. Johns*. Gainesville: Regent Press and Publishing Co., 1978.

Graham, Thomas. *The Awakening of St. Augustine: The Anderson Family and the Oldest City*. St. Augustine: St. Augustine Historical Society, 1978.

Grunwald, Michael. *The Swamp: The Everglades, Florida, and the Politics of Paradise*. New York: Simon and Schuster, 2006.

Hedrick, Joan D. *Harriet Beecher Stowe: A Life*. New York: Oxford University Press, 1994.

Hildreth, Margaret Holbrook. *Harriet Beecher Stowe: a Bibliography*. Hamden, Conn., Archon Books, 1976.

Hollis, Tom. *The Selling the Sunshine State: A Celebration of Florida Tourism Advertising*. Gainesville: University Press of Florida, 2008.

Hoyt, J. K. "From Florida." Newark, New Jersey, *Sentinel of Freedom*, June 1, 1875.

Johnson, James Weldon. *Along This Way: The Autobiography of James Weldon Johnson*. New York: Da Capo Books, 2000.

Maples, William R., and Michael Browning. *Dead Men Do Tell Tales: The Strange and Fascinating Cases of a Forensic Anthropologist*. New York: Doubleday, 1994.

Minutes of the Newark Conference of the Methodist Episcopal Church 1876. New York, 1876.

Roberts, Diane. *Dream State: Eight Generations of Swamp Lawyers, Conquistadors, Confederate Daughters, Banana Republicans, and Other Florida Wildlife*. Gainesville: University Press of Florida, 2004.

Robinson, Solon. "Florida. The Florida Home of Mrs. Stowe—Live Oaks—Sugar Cane—Ripe Strawberries." *New York Tribune*, March 5, 1868.

Shofner, Jerrell H. *Nor is It Over Yet: Florida in the Era of Reconstruction*. Gainesville: University Press of Florida, 1974.

Stowe, Charles Edward. *Life of Harriet Beecher Stowe: Compiled from Her Letters and Journals*. New York: Houghton, Mifflin, 1890.

Stowe, Harriet Beecher. "Amateur Missionaries for Florida." *Christian Union*,

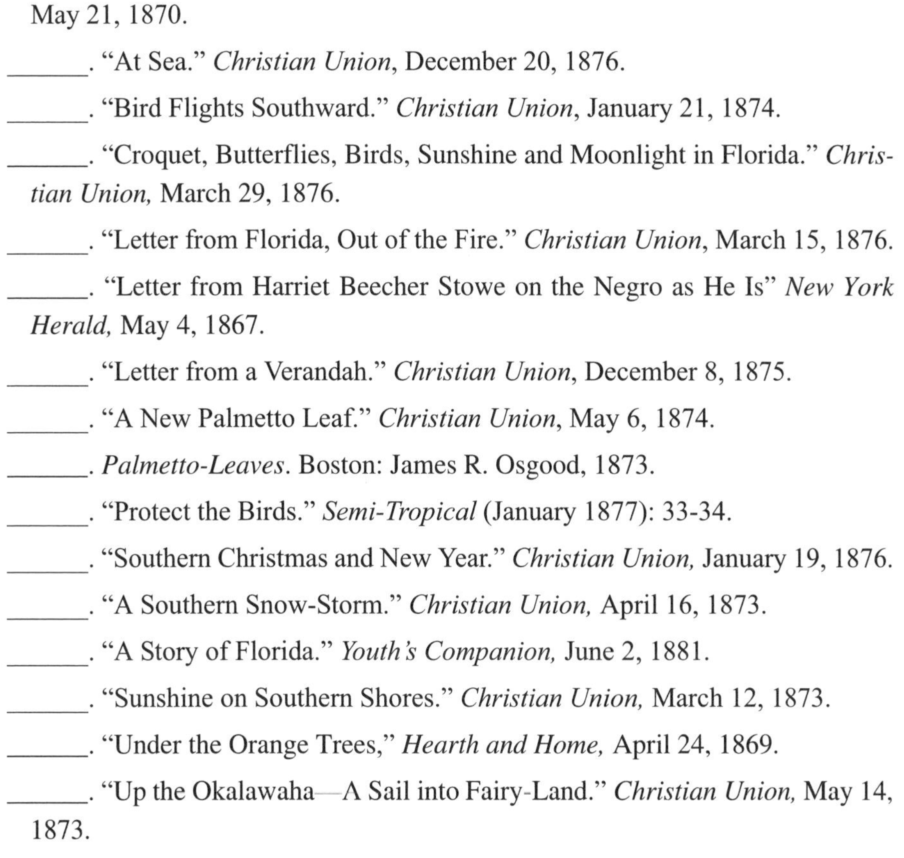

May 21, 1870.

______. "At Sea." *Christian Union*, December 20, 1876.

______. "Bird Flights Southward." *Christian Union*, January 21, 1874.

______. "Croquet, Butterflies, Birds, Sunshine and Moonlight in Florida." *Christian Union,* March 29, 1876.

______. "Letter from Florida, Out of the Fire." *Christian Union*, March 15, 1876.

______. "Letter from Harriet Beecher Stowe on the Negro as He Is" *New York Herald,* May 4, 1867.

______. "Letter from a Verandah." *Christian Union*, December 8, 1875.

______. "A New Palmetto Leaf." *Christian Union*, May 6, 1874.

______. *Palmetto-Leaves*. Boston: James R. Osgood, 1873.

______. "Protect the Birds." *Semi-Tropical* (January 1877): 33-34.

______. "Southern Christmas and New Year." *Christian Union,* January 19, 1876.

______. "A Southern Snow-Storm." *Christian Union,* April 16, 1873.

______. "A Story of Florida." *Youth's Companion,* June 2, 1881.

______. "Sunshine on Southern Shores." *Christian Union,* March 12, 1873.

______. "Under the Orange Trees," *Hearth and Home,* April 24, 1869.

______. "Up the Okalawaha—A Sail into Fairy-Land." *Christian Union,* May 14, 1873.

Stowe, Lyman Beecher. *Saints, Sinners, and Beechers: An American Family in the Nineteenth Century*. Indianapolis: Bobbs-Merrill, 1934.

Swaim, John S. "Letter from Florida." Newark *Sentinel of Freedom*, September 29, 1868.

Tebeau, Charlton W. and William Marina. *A History of Florida.* Coral Gables: University of Miami Press, 1999.

Thulesius, Olav. *Harriet Beecher Stowe in Florida, 1867 to 1884*. Jefferson, NC: McFarland and Company, 2001.

Turner, Gregg M. *A Journey into Florida Railroad History*. Gainesville, University Press of Florida, 2008.

Master List of Stowe's Florida Articles

Before *Palmetto-Leaves*, 1867-1870

Stowe, Harriet Beecher. "About the Florida Negro." *New York Herald*, May 4, 1867, p. 4.

________. "Amateur Missionaries for Florida." *Christian Union*, May 21, 1870.

________. "A Breeze from the South." *Hearth and Home*, March 19, 1870, pp. 200-1.

________. "Colored Labor of the South." *Hearth and Home*, July 3, 1869, pp. 440-41.

________. "Florida Again." *Hearth and Home*. May 15, 1869, pp. 328-9

________. "The Journey North." *Hearth and Home*, May 22, 1869, pp. 344-5.

________. "News from the South." *Hearth and Home*, April 3, 1869, p. 232.

________. "Traveling Manners." *Hearth and Home*, May 1869, p. 296.

________. "Under the Orange Trees: Number One." *Hearth and Home*, April 10, 1869, pp. 248-9.

________. "Under the Orange Trees: Number Two." *Hearth and Home*, April 17, 1869, p. 264.

________. "Under the Orange Trees: Number Three." *Hearth and Home*, April 24, 1869, pp. 280-81.

________. "What Shall We Raise in Florida?" *Hearth and Home*, May 8, 1869, p. 312.

________. "Who Ought to Come to Florida?" *Christian Union*, May 7, 1870.

After *Palmetto-Leaves*, 1873-1881

Stowe, Harriet Beecher. "At Sea." *Christian Union*, December 20, 1876.

________. "Bird Flights Southward." *Christian Union*, January 21, 1874, pp. 43-44.

________. "A Breath from the Orange Grove." *Christian Union*, Feb. 26, 1873, pp. 161-62.

________. "Croquet, Butterflies, Birds, Sunshine and Moonlight in Florida." *Christian Union,* March 29, 1876.

________. "The Florida Hegira." *Christian Union*, Dec. 2, 1874.

________. "From Florida." *Christian Union*, Dec. 13, 1876, pp. 485.

________. "Indians at St. Augustine." *Christian Union*, Feb. 7, 1877, p. 345.

________. "Indians at St. Augustine." *Christian Union*, April 25, 1877, pp. 372-73.

________. "Letter from Florida." *Christian Union*, Feb. 7, 1877.

________. "Letter from Florida, Out of the Fire." *Christian Union*, March 15, 1876, pp. 211-12.

________. "Letter from a Verandah." *Christian Union*, December 8, 1875, pp. 465-66.

________. "Lily Gathering in Florida." *Christian Union*, April 19, 1876, pp. 311-12.

________. "A New Palmetto Leaf." *Christian Union*, May 6, 1874, pp. 343-44.

________. "Our Florida Plantation." *Atlantic Monthly*, May 1879, pp. 641-649.

________. "Protect the Birds." *Semi-Tropical*, January 1877, pp. 33-34.

________. "Southern Christmas and New Year." *Christian Union*, January 19, 1876, p. 44.

________. "A Southern Snow-Storm." *Christian Union*, April 16, 1873, pp. 301-02.

________. "A Story of Florida." *Youth's Companion*, June 2, 1881, pp. 203-04.

________. "Sunshine on Southern Shores." *Christian Union*, March 12, 1873, pp. 202-03.

________. "Touching Florida." *Christian Union*, August 25, 1875, 154.

________. "Up the Okalawaha—A Sail into Fairy-Land." *Christian Union*, May 14, 1873, pp. 393-94.

________. "Villa Alexandra." *Semi-Tropical*, August 1877, pp. 448-51.

Index

F

G

H

J

K

L

M

O

P

R

S

T

U